Better Homes and Gardens®

celebrate the SEASON

1998

Better Homes and Gardens® Books
Des Moines, Iowa

Better Homes and Gardens® Books
An imprint of Meredith® Books

Celebrate the Season 1998
Editor: Vicki L. Ingham
Contributing Editor: Joyce Trollope
Art Director / Graphic Designer: Marisa Dirks
Copy Chief: Catherine Hamrick
Copy and Production Editor: Terri Fredrickson
Contributing Copy Editor: Carol L. Boker
Contributing Proofreaders: Diane Doro, Deborah Morris Smith, Margaret Smith
Electronic Production Coordinator: Paula Forest
Editorial and Design Assistants: Kaye Chabot, Judy Bailey, Treesa Landry, Karen Schirm
Test Kitchen Director: Sharon Stilwell
Production Director: Douglas M. Johnston
Production Manager: Pam Kvitne
Assistant Prepress Manager: Marjorie J. Schenkelberg

Meredith® Books
Editor in Chief: James D. Blume
Design Director: Matt Strelecki
Managing Editor: Gregory H. Kayko
Executive Shelter Editor: Denise L. Caringer
Executive Food Editor: Lisa Holderness

Director, Sales & Marketing, Retail: Michael A. Peterson
Director, Sales & Marketing, Special Markets: Rita McMullen
Director, Sales & Marketing, Home & Garden Center Channel: Ray Wolf
Director, Operations: George A. Susral

Vice President, General Manager: Jamie L. Martin

Better Homes and Gardens® Magazine
Editor in Chief: Jean LemMon
Executive Interior Design Editor: Sandra S. Soria
Executive Food Editor: Nancy Byal

Meredith Publishing Group
President, Publishing Group: Christopher M. Little
Vice President, Consumer Marketing & Development: Hal Oringer

Meredith Corporation
Chairman and Chief Executive Officer: William T. Kerr

Chairman of the Executive Committee: E. T. Meredith III

All of us at Better Homes and Gardens® Books are dedicated to providing you with information and ideas to enhance your home. We welcome your comments and suggestions. Write to us at: Better Homes and Gardens® Books, Shelter Editorial Department, 1716 Locust St., Des Moines, IA 50309-3023.

If you would like to order additional copies of this book, call 800/439-7159.

Cover photograph: Bill Holt

Our seal assures you that every recipe in *Celebrate the Season* has been tested in the Better Homes and Gardens® Test Kitchen. This means that each recipe is practical and reliable and meets our high standards of taste appeal. We guarantee your satisfaction with this book for as long as you own it.

traditions:

I have a friend who insists on hanging similar ornaments in groups on the tree, rather than distributing them evenly as I do. Another friend introduced me long ago to her practice of stuffing stockings on Christmas Eve: Each person fills someone else's handknitted stocking with a whimsical combination of silly joke gifts, practical items, and special presents that have been accumulated over the year. (The best gift goes in the toe.) Traditions like these are the touchstone of holiday celebrations, and the pleasure of the season comes in large part from anticipating them. Variety adds spice, too, and that's where this book comes in. Packed with new decorating ideas, new party recipes, and new gift projects, it's guaranteed to help you get ready for the holidays. There's something for every schedule, from instant gifts and last-minute decorations to lavish desserts and handcrafted accessories. Let these ideas complement and enhance your family's favorite customs and you're sure to create memorable celebrations this year.

Vicki Ingham

— Vicki Ingham, Editor

3

4

On the Cover

■ Pint-size potted conifers like this European cypress can come indoors for a week or so during the holidays, then go outdoors to fill a blank spot in the landscape. Ask your local nursery to suggest a suitable variety of juniper, spruce, cypress, or pine. Place the tree in a cool, sunny window and water it often enough to keep the soil smoist but not soggy. To prevent problems with spider mites, remove the decorations about midweek and give the tree a cool, gentle shower. After Christmas, place the tree in the garage or on an unheated porch for a couple of weeks to let it readjust to the outdoors.

table *of* contents

setting the stage

gathering together

giving from the heart

5

kids' stuff

In a Twinkling
Easy-to-use ideas for the holidays

Dressing your house in festive finery sets the stage for a glorious season of celebration. Starting at the entrance and enlivening every room, decorations create a happy atmosphere that marks this time of year—and your home—as special. Some elements are standard: For Christmas, a wreath on the door, a tree in the family room, and a Nativity on the mantel embrace the traditional symbols, while a menorah is essential for Hanukkah. Beyond the basics, however, you can add colorful accessories, such as easy-to-sew pillow slipcovers, lampshade "necklaces," and quick holiday valances, to transform a room instantly and dramatically. Time is at a premium during the holidays, so we've selected projects that you can complete easily, some of them at the last minute. You may need to visit a crafts store or floral supply shop to find some of the materials, but you won't need to take a crash course in crafting to complete the projects.

SETTING

*the*STAGE

Extend a cheerful holiday welcome with a wreath that reflects your personal style. Mix natural materials for a rustic look, or choose apples and plaid ribbon for traditional and country settings. For a touch of whimsy, use vegetables instead of fruit.

wreathed in
splendor

Start with a purchased fresh wreath—or use an artificial one and add sprigs of whatever live greenery is available. Just tuck the cut greens among the wired branches, bending and shaping the branches to hold the material in place. A third option (see *pages 10–11*) is to make your own fresh wreath, using a foam wreath form from a floral supply shop.

nature's wreath

here's how...

1 To make a wreath like the one shown on *page 7*, collect fallen pieces of birch bark or sycamore bark, twigs, cones, and shelf fungus from the woods or your yard. If you can't find shelf fungus, look for "shelf mushrooms" in the dried flower department of a crafts store. Each "mushroom," which is actually a fungus, is glued to a long wooden pick, which you can snip off with pruning shears.

2 Arrange the largest items in the bottom right quadrant of the wreath for a focal point. Use a hot-glue gun to attach the materials (see *page 156* for tips on using glue guns). Glue materials of similar size at the 9 o'clock position for visual balance. Add dried pomegranates (available in crafts stores) and dried apple slices around the front and inside edges of the wreath. Wire a red velvet bow to the top right quadrant.

apples and plaids

here's how...

1 To make the bow, cut the ribbon into two 42-inch pieces, two 24-inch pieces, and one 28-inch piece. Fold each of the 42-inch pieces to make three loops of graduated lengths, keeping the bottoms of the loops even. Cut a V-shaped notch through all fabric layers at the bottom to eliminate some of the bulk, then wire the base of the loops to a floral pick (see the inset photo on *page 9*). Fold each of the 24-inch lengths to make a 6-inch loop with a 12-inch streamer and wire it to a floral pick. Fold the 28-inch piece in half to make a 2-inch loop with streamers and wire it to a floral pick.

2 Insert the triple loops on each side of the wreath's center top. Shape the loops to resemble a large bow nestled among the greenery. Insert the loops with streamers on each side of the center bow, and add the loop with two streamers at the center (this is the knot).

3 Glue magnolia leaves to the top half of the wreath. Wire the apples among the bow loops (see *page 157* for instructions on wiring apples). Glue walnuts and pinecones to the front of the wreath as shown on *page 9*.

Save on ribbon but achieve the look of
a full, fluffy bow with this technique.
Fold ribbon to make one, two,
or three loops. Notch the
ribbon at the bottom of the
loops to reduce bulk; wire
the loops to wooden
floral picks and insert.

9

SHOPPING LIST

FOR APPLES AND PLAIDS
purchased 24-inch-diameter
    fresh wreath
6-inch wooden floral picks
medium-gauge floral wire
4½ yards of
    2¼-inch-wide
    wire-edge ribbon
15 magnolia leaves (fresh,
    preserved, or silk)
8 pinecones
3 fresh or latex apples
8 to 10 walnuts
hot-glue gun and
    glue sticks

10

Harvest Home

Hang this wreath for Thanksgiving, then give it a Christmas accent with a big red bow.

The potatoes and onions will last at least a month, and the corn will dry in place. You may need to replace the carrots after about a week. It's easy to make repairs if critters find the vegetables irresistible: Just pull out the nibbled pieces and insert fresh ones on bamboo skewers.

1 Use pruning shears or utility scissors to cut off the handle of the basket. Push the handle ends into the front of the wreath form at the top to make a perch for birds.

2 Use floral wire to attach the basket to the front of the wreath form at the bottom.

freshness counts

Check a wreath for freshness as you would a Christmas tree. Shake it gently to make sure it doesn't drop needles. Bend a branch tip between your fingers to see if the needles are firm but pliable, and give the wreath the sniff test—it should smell strongly fragrant.

Wreaths made from freshly cut evergreens should last up to a month (fir will last even longer). Since cool temperatures and high humidity help keep the greenery in good condition, outdoor locations are perfect for displaying wreaths.

3 Cut the stem ends of fresh greenery at an angle to make a point. Starting at the top and working toward the bottom, insert the stem ends into one-half of the foam wreath base, making sure the stem ends all point in the same direction. Repeat to cover the other half.

4 Use bamboo skewers or wooden floral picks to attach the vegetables to the wreath, referring to the photo on *page 10* for placement. Fill in around the vegetables with additional greenery and pinecones. Fill the basket with nuts.

Gather the gifts of the forest to decorate your home. Leaves, pinecones, twigs, and bark bring nature's textures indoors to warm your rooms with elegant simplicity.

decorations
from nature

❧ To make the decorations shown on the following pages, you can collect most of the natural materials you'll need from your own yard. However, avoid collecting moss from the woods; instead, buy packages of sheet moss, sphagnum moss, or Spanish moss from crafts stores or floral supply shops. These commercially available products will be free of insects and dry enough to accept glue. And, you won't be damaging natural stands, which can be slow-growing and difficult to replenish.

moss balls
here's how...

Start with plastic foam balls from a crafts store. Coat each ball with thick white crafts glue and press sheet moss or sphagnum moss firmly into the glue. Hold the moss in place with toothpicks until the glue dries. Repeat this procedure until you've covered the ball entirely with moss. Wrap the ball with fine gold cord as if you were winding a ball of yarn, securing the ends with dressmaker's pins.

SHOPPING LIST

From a crafts store:
miniature basket
hot-glue gun and glue
    sticks
floral foam (optional)
sheet moss
raffia
white spray paint
narrow red satin ribbon
rubber bands

From your yard:
holly sprigs
laurel leaves or
    other broad-leaf
    evergreens, such
    as pittosporum,
    photinia, or bay (also
    available from a florist)
¾-inch-thick branch
large pinecone
dried leaves and shelf
    fungus

From a florist's shop:
florist's water vial
fresh rose

14

Natural Tree Trims

Highlight your tree with baskets, bouquets, and pendants of nature's materials.

❧ To get the most impact from these ornaments, make 5 to 10 of each and distribute them evenly over the tree. Enhance the theme with other items you may have on hand—oyster shells, moss balls, and pieces of driftwood add interest with a variety of shapes and textures. To unify the various items, use red ribbon to tie the ornaments to the tree. Add clear glass balls to catch the light and lend sparkling textural contrast to the natural materials.

family traditions

When my two sisters and I were in our teens, my family began a tradition of having an indoor picnic on Christmas Eve instead of a big dinner. This was especially fun since we were living in the Midwest and were usually surrounded by snow and ice. We'd get special kosher hot dogs, potato salad, and all the picnic accoutrements; cook the hot dogs in the fireplace; and eat while sitting on a blanket. We'd end a comfortable, casual evening by going to the candlelight service.

— *Ruth A. Baldrige*
Charlotte, North Carolina

rose basket

Attach sprigs of holly to the edges of a miniature basket with hot glue. Or, glue a small piece of floral foam into the basket and insert the holly stems into it. Clip the stem of the rose to about 3 inches. Fill the florist's water vial with water, replace the rubber cap, and insert the rose's stem through the hole in the cap. Place the rose in the basket—the weight of the vial should hold it in position. Fill the basket with a pad of sheet moss to hide the vial.

pinecone pendant

Use garden loppers to cut a ¾-inch-thick branch into a 4- or 5-inch-long section. Randomly tuck pieces of moss under the scales of a large pinecone and work a piece of raffia under the scales around the bottom of the cone. Knot the raffia to secure it, then tie the raffia ends around the branch and knot the ends to form a 3- or 4-inch-long hanging loop. Use a hot-glue gun to attach dried leaves, shelf fungus, or other embellishments to the pinecone.

timesaving tip

If you don't have much time to decorate, concentrate your efforts in two areas—the one that guests see first and the one where you spend the most time. If you have an entry foyer, create a tabletop display like the one shown on *page 16*. If the staircase is the first thing guests see when they come in, swag it with garland and decorate the newel post.

laurel leaf bouquet

Spray fresh laurel leaves (or other broad-leaf evergreen leaves as suggested in the Shopping List on *page 14*) with white spray paint. Bundle several stems together with a rubber band, then wrap narrow red satin ribbon over the rubber band. Tie the ribbon in a knot; cut the ends to the desired length, and knot them to form the hanging loop.

15

here's how...

16

Gilded Garland

Wire together oak leaves and wooden acorns to drape over a mirror or along the edge of a mantel.

SHOPPING LIST

From your yard:
dried leaves

From a crafts store:
wooden acorns
jewelry eye pins
thick white crafts glue
gold spray paint

From a hardware store:
sandpaper
16- and 20-gauge
brass wire

〜 This garland turns a tabletop display into a holiday vignette. Place moss-covered balls on the table, on pedestals, and at the base of a purchased topiary (see *page 12* for instructions on making the moss balls). Add dried pomegranates and gold-painted walnuts and acorns. An antique Santa's sleigh and reindeer add charm here. Other seasonal accents you could use include vintage ornaments piled in glass bowls or a plate of fruit (fresh or fake) treated with gold leaf— see *page 45* for how to apply gold leaf.

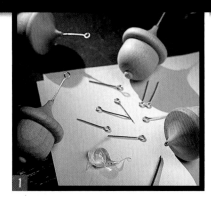

Sand off the point on the cap of each wooden acorn and use a nail to make a small hole in the sanded end. Glue an eye pin into the hole.

Place the acorns in a box and spray them with gold spray paint. After the paint dries, shake the box gently to roll the acorns, exposing their unpainted sides. Spray again; repeat this procedure until the acorns are covered completely. Spray-paint the leaves gold, too.

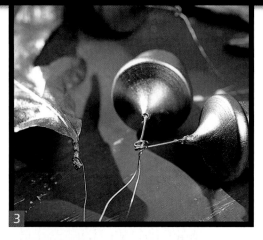

Use 20-gauge brass wire to connect the acorns. Also wrap the stems of the leaves with wire, leaving a 2- or 3-inch extension for connecting the leaf to the garland.

To make the wire garland, attach doubled 16-gauge wire to the beater of an electric hand mixer. Wrap the other ends of the wire around a pencil, and turn the mixer on, using a slow speed. The beater will automatically twist the wire into a cord.

Attach the leaves and acorn clusters to the wire garland by wrapping the extension wires around the garland wire.

17

18

Forest Topiary

Use a single topiary as a centerpiece or make a pair for the mantel.

〰 Gilded leaves and dried pomegranates give this mossy, fresh-from-the-forest tree a natural holiday accent. For a slicker, more contemporary look, omit the leaves and use frosted glass balls instead of the pinecones and pomegranates. Or, cover the topiary entirely with white and pink seashells of various sizes to use in a beach home year-round.

1

Mix the plaster of Paris with water according to the package directions. Pour the mixture into the pot, and center the dowel in it. To hold the dowel upright while the plaster sets, make a grid of masking tape across the top of the pot. Let the plaster harden completely.

3

Using a hot-glue gun, glue sheet moss to the chicken wire and over the top of the pot to hide the plaster.

19

2

Roll the chicken wire lengthwise to form a tube, then bend it in a spiral around the dowel. Flatten the tip to form a point.

4

Glue the pinecones and pomegranates in the spaces between the spirals, clustering them in groups of twos and threes for more impact. Add the leaves so they look like they've just fallen on the forest floor. Glue puffs of reindeer moss over the sheet moss for contrasting texture.

◀ Emphasize favorite artwork with crowns of greenery. Simply tuck branches behind the frame; the frame's weight will hold the boughs in place.

▼ Quickly transform a homemade or purchased grapevine wreath by adding apples and a few sprigs of pine or fir. Weave the stem ends of the greens into the grapevine to secure them. To attach the apples, wire them in place with floral wire (see *page 157*).

In a Twinkling:
Decorations

20

◀ Fill a large copper pot or wooden bucket with fresh fir and cedar to bring holiday aroma to a hearth or entry. Stack blocks of floral foam or crafts foam in the container so you can position the stems where you want them. Skewer oranges on sticks or long floral picks, and insert them among the greenery.

If you collect creamware, silver, porcelain, or majolica, display it on a garland for the holidays. Make sure the mirror or painting frame is firmly attached to the wall so it can support the weight. The garland should rest securely on the frame, too. Use raffia to tie the serving pieces in place.

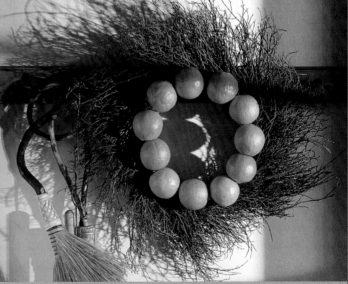

Untwist the top of a coat hanger and thread oranges onto the wire. Use medium-gauge floral wire to fasten the fruit ring onto a purchased twig wreath.

Lift the eye with branches of cedar, juniper, pine, or other evergreens on the chandelier. Tie the branches in place with floral wire.

It's the centerpiece of every holiday home, but you don't need to limit yourself to just one. Themed or specialty trees give a lift to every room in your house.

O christmas tree!

Tabletop Tree

～ If you don't have room for a floor-to-ceiling tree, try a short, fat tabletop tree instead. The one shown here has been nailed to a thick slice of wood for a natural base. Grapevines make a freeform garland, which wraps randomly through the branches. Blown-glass pinecone ornaments accompany real pinecones dipped in white paint. For instructions on how to turn inexpensive red glass balls into snow-dipped ornaments, see *page 24*. (To create a "clothesline" for drying the ornaments, tie a length of jute between two sturdy supports, making sure the line is taut.)

keeping your tree fresh

■ When you bring your tree home, cut about ¼ inch off the bottom of the trunk, cutting on the diagonal to expose a larger area to absorb water. Place the trunk in a bucket of water in a garage or basement where it will be protected from freezing temperatures.

■ When you're ready to set the tree up, cut another ¼ inch off the bottom, making a straight cut this time so the tree will be stable in the stand. Check the water reservoir daily—a 6-foot-tall tree can drink up to a gallon of water in the first 24 hours and 2 quarts of water a day thereafter.

SHOPPING LIST

white crafts paint or latex
   interior paint
waxed paper or paper plate
sea sponge
scrap paper
red glass-ball ornaments
jute string

family traditions

For as long as I can remember, my family has celebrated St. Nicholas Day, December 6. We hang our stockings for that day rather than for Christmas, as was the custom in Germany, the home of my ancestors. My husband and I have continued the tradition with our children and now our grandchild. It's like having a bit of Christmas early, and I sometimes think they enjoy those stocking presents and the early celebration more than the "big day."

— *Marilyn Schmidt*
Kennebunkport, Maine

24

Snow-Dipped Ornaments

here's how...

1 Pour a small amount of white paint onto a piece of waxed paper or a paper plate.

2 Dip a dampened sea sponge into the paint, then pat it on a piece of scrap paper to remove the excess paint. Pat the sponge onto an ornament, being careful not to cover the ball entirely. Tie a length of jute between two supports and hang the ball to dry.

3 For a solid-snow effect, submerge the bottom half of an ornament in the paint, holding the ball at an angle. Let the excess paint drip back into the can. Hang the ornament to dry.

Blanket of Snow

∾ To create a convincing effect of thick snow *(below)*, lay lengths of rolled cotton along the branches. Sprinkle crystal snow over the cotton.

25

The Well-Dressed Tree

∾ Straw hats and kid gloves dress this tree *(above)*. You don't need a whole hat collection to adapt the idea—two or three strategically placed bonnets will do the trick. The same holds true for the gloves. Add ribbon streamers and clusters of dried hydrangeas to evoke a garden-party feeling.

Tea for Two

❧ Almost anything is fair game when it comes to creating a themed tree. If you have a collection of mismatched tea cups and spoons, tie them to the branches with ribbons. You can even glue cups to their saucers with dots of hot glue (the cups can be gently pried from the saucers and the glue popped off after the holidays). Check specialty Christmas shops for ornaments in the shape of cakes and petits fours. For a Victorian accent, weave lengths of lace among the branches.

Hydrangea Bouquets

To suggest the effect of snow, nestle clusters of dried hydrangea on your tree branches. For a garland, swag lengths of gold drapery cording in asymmetrical loops and weave gold-mesh wire-edge ribbon among the branches. Pinch and crimp the ribbon so it traces an interesting, meandering line through the boughs.

Country Inspiration

Add contrasting texture and color to your tree by inserting broad-leaf evergreens among the boughs. In mild-winter areas, collect magnolia, elaeagnus, mahonia, or nandina from your yard to soften the look of an artificial tree. On a fresh, less-than-perfect specimen, these branches effectively fill holes and help balance the shape. If you don't have access to broad-leaf evergreens, purchase salal or eucalyptus from a florist or collect branchlets of dried oak leaves or beech leaves and spray them gold, copper, and silver.

To duplicate the oversize red mittens, start with plain red oven mitts. Stitch or glue wide ribbon at the opening to make a cuff. Attach a Santa ornament and a bow.

Collect miniature bottles, such as antique or reproduction medicine bottles or recycled flavoring bottles. Partially fill them with water. Tie narrow ribbon tightly around the neck. Slip floral wire under the ribbon, and wire the bottle to the tree. Insert one or two stems of fresh flowers. Use a small funnel to add water every other day.

In a Twinkling: Ornaments

String together dried orange slices using raffia and a large-eye tapestry needle. To dry your own oranges, cut slices ¼ inch thick and place them on a baking sheet in an oven set to 200° for 6 to 10 hours; or use a food dehydrator according to the manufacturer's instructions.

Look for old wooden spools silk buttonhole-twist thread or bu wooden spools at a crafts store wrap colorful thread around the Sandwich each spool between s wooden car wheels and woode beads from a crafts store, then th the hanging cord of a purchased tassel through the beads, wheels and spool.

◀ Check flea markets and antiques shops for chandelier crystals. Thread a wire through the crystal's hanging wire if necessary, and twist it to make a loop. Use ribbon to tie the loop to the tree branch.

Look for old or new pin cushions in novelty shapes. Use a needle and doubled thread to tack a ribbon-loop hanger to the top of the pin cushion. Glue a knotted ribbon over the tacked area. Dip the ends of quilting pins in white glue; insert them into the pincushion. ▶

◀ Show off collectible spoons by tying them with bows and wiring them to the tree. To avoid scratching the spoons, use green cotton-covered florist's wire, available from floral supply shops or crafts stores.

If the job of lighting the Christmas tree makes you reach for the aspirin bottle, here's help. Bob Pranga and Debi Staron, the professional tree-decorating team known as Dr. Christmas, show how to light your tree efficiently and beautifully—and, hopefully, with fewer headaches.

lighting
made
easier

✍ Creating a magical glow of lights on an artificial tree isn't difficult but demands patience; on a fresh tree, it calls for both patience and a trick of the trade described on *page 32*.

Bob Pranga developed his lighting and decorating techniques while he was working as a designer in a Christmas shop in New York City. His talents were so much in demand that he gave up aspirations of becoming an actor and devoted himself fulltime to developing a professional holiday decorating and consulting service. One customer dubbed him Dr. Christmas because of the 24-hour emergency service and house calls he provided, and the name

stuck. After several years, Debi Staron joined him, and they moved the business to California, where they've become known as "tree stylists to the stars." The duo has produced a series of informative videos on buying, lighting, and decorating fresh and artificial trees (for ordering information, call 310/854-0886).

■ *Lighting a fresh tree: We used an artificial tree and lights on a white cord so you can see clearly how the cords weave back and forth in a triangular shape.*

plug it in

Christmas tree lights are either stacked (the white plugs *above*) or end to end, also called string to string (the green plugs *above*). Check the boxes of lights before you buy to make sure they're all compatible. Bob and Debi recommend stacked plugs because you can join more strands than you can with end-to-end type plugs. Be sure to check the box for the manufacturer's recommendations, however. Usually you can string together three 100-light strands or six 50-light strands.

how many lights?

For a fresh tree, plan on three 100-light sets per tree foot.

For an artificial tree, Dr. Christmas recommends using 50-light strands: the 100-light strands are two 50-light strands wired together, and the 50-light strands are easier to work with as you wrap the tree branches. In addition, the 50-light sets are less likely to burn out or have electrical problems. For subdued lighting, use about 12 boxes for a 6-foot tree and about 20 boxes for an 8-foot tree. For moderate lighting, use 20 boxes for a 6-foot tree and 30 boxes for an 8-foot tree. For showcase lighting, use 40 boxes and 80 boxes respectively.

lighting a fresh tree

Instead of wrapping the lights around the tree in a maypole dance, Bob and Debi suggest that you mentally divide the tree into three triangular sections.

Plug in the first string of lights and nestle the last bulb on the string at the top of the tree next to the trunk. Weave the lights back and forth across the triangle, being careful not to cross the cord over itself. When you reach the end of the first string, plug in the next set and continue weaving the lights back and forth until you reach the bottom, connecting no more than 300 lights end to end. Repeat this procedure for the remaining triangles.

Step back from the tree and look at it with your eyes crossed. Wherever you see dark holes on the tree, rearrange the lights as necessary to fill in. To remove the lights without getting them tangled, simply work in reverse.

lighting an artificial tree

The artificial trees available today come in sections that open like an umbrella. If you use miniature lights, you can wrap them around the branches and leave them on permanently. Just be sure to light each section separately (that is, don't cross a section or point of assembly with a strand of lights).

FOR SUBDUED LIGHTING, begin at the bottom of the tree close to the trunk. Allowing some slack or leader cord in the first strand of lights, separate the cord near the first bulb so it forms a loop. Slip the loop over one of the branchlets or "greens" near the trunk, and wrap the cord a few times around the green to secure it (see Photo 1). Pull the string of lights taut to the tip of the branch, then work back toward the trunk, wrapping the cord over itself and the branch (see Photo 2). Separate the cord again when you reach the trunk, and slip the cord over a branchlet to secure it. Carry the cord over to the next branch, wrap it around a green near the trunk, and pull it out to the tip. Wrap the cord over itself and the branch as before. Continue wrapping branches in this manner until you come to the end of the string. Plug in the next set, and keep going until you reach the point where the tree comes apart. Work any extra lights back along the branch rather than crossing the section. When you wrap the top section of the tree, don't wrap the lights around as many branches so the tree will look evenly lit from top to bottom.

FOR MODERATE LIGHTING, follow the same procedure, but wrap the cord around some of the greens along the branch as you work back toward the trunk (see Photo 3).

FOR SHOWCASE LIGHTING, wrap the cord around every green as you work back along the branch.

outdoor lights

- If you floodlight evergreens outdoors, use white, blue, or green lamps; red, yellow, amber, and pink lamps will make the trees look a muddy brown.

- Don't try to hang strings of lights from the eaves with cuphooks—in a strong wind, the wires may swing loose. Instead, use plastic gutter clips that hook onto the gutter and hold the wire tightly in place. Look for packages of gutter clips in crafts stores and hardware stores with the tree lights and supplies.

- Be sure you have outdoor electrical sockets to plug into when you use outdoor lights.

- Don't worry about hiding the electrical cords—just keep them organized neatly, and no one will notice them.

here's how...

Slip the loop over one of the branchlets or "greens" near the trunk to secure it.

Pull the string of lights out to the tip of the branch, then wrap the cord around itself and the branch as you work back toward the trunk.

For moderate lighting, wrap the cord around some of the greens along the branch as you work back toward the trunk. For showcase lighting, wrap the cord around every green.

If you don't need to use your fireplace to help heat your home, try filling the firebox with pillar candles of all sizes. You'll get the effect of firelight without the mess of wood ashes! Add fresh greenery and gilded leaves, but be sure to keep plant materials well away from the candles' flames.

In a Twinkling: Candles

◀ To make old-fashioned sugared fruit (for display only), brush fruit with egg white, then roll each piece in superfine sugar. This technique is best used for a special occasion—after a couple of days, the sugar may begin to absorb moisture from the air and won't look its best.

Note: Never leave burning candles unattended.

◀ Enhance the cozy effect of a fire by grouping pillar candles in front of the hearth. To display them, half-fill a terra-cotta planter with sand and stand the candles in the sand.

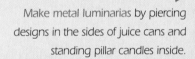 Make metal luminarias by piercing designs in the sides of juice cans and standing pillar candles inside.

◀ Canning jars make wonderful country-style candleholders. Half-fill them with sand and wedge a candle down into the sand. Tie a sprig of cedar and berries around each jar's mouth with twine.

Ward off winter's chill and create an inviting setting for friends and family with a few simple decorating techniques. Fragrance, light, and furniture arrangement can evoke a warm mood.

cozy up
your rooms

a fresh point of view

A room's focal point catches the eye and draws you into the room. It also anchors the furnishings. A fireplace serves this purpose, but so can windows with a beautiful view or a wall lined with books. For the holidays, the tree usually takes center stage in the living room or family room. To give it the most impact, pair it with the room's natural focus, rearranging the furniture if necessary to spotlight the tree. Place the sofa on the diagonal, for example, to take in both the tree and the fireplace. Bracket the sofa with chairs and side tables to create a close-knit grouping for conversation.

snug as a bug

To enhance the feeling of congenial coziness, draw chairs and sofa closer together. A space of about 18 inches between the sofa and cocktail table or between chairs is enough for people to move comfortably into the inner circle.

silent butler

Make sure each seating piece has a place nearby for guests to set their drinks. This can be a side table, cocktail table, a stack of large books, a pedestal, or a glass-topped urn. It just needs to be about the same height as the arm of the seating piece.

a warm sweater

Pull textured furnishings and accessories around your conversation spot like a sweater. Chenille or wool throws, plump holiday pillows, and layered rugs create an inviting warmth that coaxes you to linger.

good scents

Fragrance creates a holiday mood. Choose from the many potpourris and scented candles available commercially, or make your own simmering potpourri by adding powdered cinnamon and citrus peels to water in a saucepan. Keep it on the stove on the lowest possible heat, and add water as necessary. Remember to turn the heat off before you leave home or go to bed.

building traditions

It's a fact that many people face the prospect of spending the holidays alone. To cope with this, I have developed a number of strategies over the years that have made the holidays not only *not* lonely but also meaningful and enjoyable. These include cultivating true friendships, baby-sitting for couples with small children during the year, keeping in touch with my married sisters and brothers (and working hard at being a good guest), inviting others to my home to celebrate with me, and volunteering with local organizations that take care of the needy. As a result, I'm "(Not) Home Alone" for the holidays. These strategies may not work for everyone, but I believe the principle can apply to every life, that in giving of ourselves to others, we also receive.

— *Diane Krantz*
Ogden, Utah

let it glow

Soft, sparkling light enhances the holiday mood. Lower the wattage in table lamps, and supplement them with small decorative lamps, picture lights over artwork, and candles. Create a glowing centerpiece for a table by wrapping strings of lights around a grapevine wreath that you've sprayed white. (Use lights on a white cord.) Nest a glass bowl inside the wreath, and lay more lights inside the bowl. Then fill the bowl with clear glass orbs, ornaments, and stars.

If the decoration sits on an end table or in an entry, you can use plug-in lights. Otherwise you'll need to use battery-operated ones.

Mesh Candleholders

To create votive holders similar to those shown here, wrap small jars with bronze screening available from a hardware store.

You can recycle baby food jars or other small glass containers to hold the candles, or use straight-sided votive candleholders. Group the candles with other metallic objects, such as gilded balls and burnished vases, which will reflect the light and create a warm glow. The screening isn't sharp, but the cut edges can be prickly so you may want to wear gloves while working.

SHOPPING LIST

pliers, scissors, compass
small jar
heavy rubber band
votive candle or tea light
From a hardware store:
   bronze screening
   18-gauge brass wire

here's how...

To figure the radius of the circle for the screening, multiply the height of the jar by two, then add the diameter of the bottom plus 2 inches. Divide this measurement in half and set the compass to the resulting figure. Or tie a piece of string to a pencil, cut the string to the length of the radius, and pin the other end to the paper. Draw a circle on a piece of scrap paper. Using the paper circle as a pattern, cut a circle from the screening. Mark the center of the screen circle by folding it in half and then in half again. Open the screen out, and center the jar on the circle.

Fold the screening up around the jar, and temporarily hold it in place around the jar's neck with a heavy rubber band. Pinch the bottom edges and corners to give the container a boxy shape. Wrap brass wire around the neck, and twist it tightly with pliers. Shape the excess screening as desired to make a flange or collar. Remove the rubber band and insert the votive candle or tea light.

39

did you know?

Poinsettias are native to Mexico, where the Aztecs grew them for dye and medicine. The name honors Joel Poinsett, U.S. ambassador to Mexico from 1825 to 1829. An amateur botanist, he brought the plants home to South Carolina and began propagating them in his greenhouse. Although the leaves aren't poisonous, they can cause stomach discomfort if ingested, so keep plants out of the reach of young children and pets.

Create holiday drama with seasonal touches that emphasize your home's architecture. And fill the house with festive spirit by dressing up accessories and furnishings you enjoy year-round.

festive
finishing
touches

✍ A staircase makes an instant focal point. All you have to do is add greenery and bright poinsettias to establish a holiday mood.

Fresh garland is usually made by wiring individual branches to a heavy base wire or to twine or rope. A wire base is less flexible, so for closely spaced swags on a staircase, look for garland made on a rope or twine base. For one deep loop, like the swag shown here, a wire base works fine. Before you buy the garland, test the way it droops to make sure you like the effect.

To determine how much garland you need, tie heavy clothesline or twine to the top of the stair rail. Drape the clothesline along the stair in the desired number of swags and wrap it around the newel post. Add a couple of feet to allow for the garland's thickness.

here's how...

Fasten purchased garland to the stair rail with green chenille wire, which won't scratch the woodwork and will blend with the greenery. Look for chenille wires in crafts stores—they're like pipe cleaners, but they come in longer lengths and a variety of colors. After you've wired the garland in place, use floral wire to attach branches of red berries, such as holly, possum haw, winterberry, or yaupon holly, to the greenery. Or, use canella berries, available at crafts stores. Add dried salal leaves for contrasting texture and tone.

Evergreen Cornice

Crown your windows with bow ties of greenery to lift the eye and emphasize a view of the outdoors.

SHOPPING LIST

From a florist, a garden center, or your yard:
branches of fir or
hemlock (or
substitute pine)
branches of berried
juniper
salal
stems of assorted herbs

From a crafts store:
spool wire
canella berries or
rose hips
18-inch-long cinnamon
sticks
raffia

here's how...

This cornice is easy to make by wiring boughs together with the ends overlapping. Layering herbs, rose hips, and cinnamon sticks over the evergreens creates a classic country-style swag. For a more formal look, substitute seeded eucalyptus (available from a florist) and dried roses for the herbs and rose hips, and bind the bow tie with wide satin ribbon.

To hang the swag, tap two small nails into the top of the window frame or into the wall just above it, spacing them an equal distance from the center. Slip the swag's hanging wires over the nails.

1. Cut the fir branches to a little more than half the width of your window frame. Divide the branches into two groups. Lay the stems end to end, overlapping them several inches, and bind the branches together tightly with spool wire.

2. Cut the juniper branches so they're slightly shorter than the fir. Layer them over the fir with stem ends overlapping and wire them in place. In the same way, layer the herbs, berries, salal, and cinnamon sticks, angling the cinnamon sticks as shown in the photo. Wire each layer of materials in place.

3. Tie raffia tightly over the center of the swag, knotting it at the front. To attach hanging wires, place the swag facedown, and wrap wire around a sturdy branch on each side, aligned with the nails in the window frame or wall. Wrap the wires around the nails, adjusting the lengths as necessary.

43

Accent on Accessories

Work holiday magic with decorative details.

From a fabric store:
   ½ yard of 56-inch-wide
      upholstery fabric
   fusible interfacing
   tassels
   beading needle or
      very fine needle
   thread to match fabric
From a crafts store:
   foil adhesive
   foam brush
   composition leaf in gold,
      silver, or copper
   burnishing tool (optional)
   soft bristle brush
   seed beads
From the grocery store:
   carambolas (star fruit)

Give your rooms a new look for the season with a few simple accessories that go beyond the expected. A quick add-on valance (see *page 59* for details), lampshade trims, a table runner, and pillows will help make spirits bright.

stamped table runner

here's how...

1 Cut a strip of fabric 14×56 inches. Hem the long raw edges with a machine stitch, and press.

45

2 Fold under the fabric at each end to form a point. Press the folded edges, and tack the ends in place; or use fusible interfacing following the manufacturer's instructions.

3 To stamp the stars, work on a smooth, hard surface and place scrap paper under the fabric. Cut the star fruit in half and blot the cut surface on a paper towel. Using the foam brush, apply foil adhesive to the cut surface.

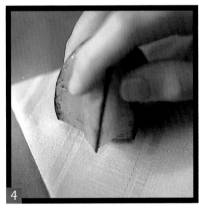

4 Starting at one end of the runner, press the fruit firmly and gently onto the fabric, making sure each point of the fruit contacts the fabric. Reapply adhesive to the fruit, and repeat the procedure several more times, placing the stars randomly. Work on one small section of the runner at a time so the adhesive doesn't get too dry. When it's tacky to the touch, gently lay a sheet of composition leaf over the adhesive.

5 Rub the composition leaf firmly and carefully with your fingernail or a burnishing tool. (If you use a burnishing tool, place a piece of heavy plastic, such as a cereal-box liner, between the tool and the leaf to keep from tearing the leaf.) Lift the leaf away from the image, and repeat this procedure to apply composition leaf to the remaining stamped stars. Brush away excess leaf with a soft bristle brush. Repeat to complete the runner. When one star fruit surface starts to wear out, cut a fresh piece of fruit. Using the beading needle and thread, sew a bead at each star point. Stitch a tassel to each end. Because the composition leaf is not washable, you may want to spray the finished runner with spray-on fabric protector; spot-clean any spills.

3

Follow the manufacturer's instructions to install the grommets. At each end, work through both layers of fabric.

4 Center the pillow on the wrong side of the towel. Wrap the folded edges over the pillow along the sides, then bring the top and bottom grommeted edges together. If necessary, make a few long handstitches from side to side to keep the folded edges in place before you bring the grommeted edges together.

place mat pillow

here's how...

1 Stack the place mats with wrong sides facing. Mark the placement for the buttons 1½ inches in from the outer edge on all sides, starting in one corner and allowing for six evenly spaced buttons on each long side and four evenly spaced on each short side.

2 Pin the place mats together on the markings and stitch with a few hand or machine stitches. Leave three marked points open along the bottom edge for inserting the pillow form.

3 Use pearl cotton or embroidery floss to sew the buttons over the stitched points. Insert the pillow form. Stitch the last three marked points together and sew the buttons over them.

tea towel pillow

here's how...

1 Press under about 3 inches along the two long sides of the towel (the design of the towel may dictate that you turn under a little more or less).

2 On the right side of the towel, about 1⅛ inches from the edge along each short end, mark the placement for six evenly spaced grommets. Reinforce the wrong side of the ends with fusible interfacing.

5

Lace ribbon through the grommets as if you were lacing a shoe; tie the ends in a bow. Or, start at opposite ends and lace toward the center as shown on page 44.

lampshade necklace

SHOPPING LIST

From a hardware store:
6 feet of brass
beaded or ball chain
beaded chain connector
wire cutters, needle-nose
pliers, round-nose
pliers

**From the jewelry-supply
department of a
crafts store:**
gold head pins
assorted crystal beads
7mm gold jump rings
assorted star charms

here's how...

1 String crystal beads of varying sizes and colors onto the head pins. Wrap the long end of the pin around the round-nose pliers to make a loop. Cut off the excess pin with the wire cutters. Squeeze the loop closed using the needle-nose pliers.

2 To attach the charms and beads to the chain, open the jump rings by separating them at the side—don't pull them apart. Slide a star charm or a string of crystal beads onto each jump ring, then squeeze the jump ring closed over the chain. Connect the ends with the chain connector. Form the chain into a double or triple loop and arrange it as desired on the lampshade.

lampshade crown

here's how...

1 Cut a length of ivy garland to fit snugly over the lampshade, either at the top or near the bottom. Pull the leaves off their plastic pegs or stubs, keeping every fourth set of leaves in place.

2 Pull leaves off the holly garland and push them onto every two or three empty stubs on the ivy garland.

3 To make the berry units, slip a bead over an eye pin. Use the round-nose pliers to curl the straight end of the pin into a "pig's tail" to keep the bead from slipping off. Clip off the excess wire. Leave 1½ to 2 inches of wire between the eye and the berry to form a stem; make the stems different lengths. Slip the eyes of one or two pins over the remaining empty plastic stubs on the ivy garland.

SHOPPING LIST

From a crafts store:
3-inch silver jewelry
eye pins
10mm red glass beads
silk ivy garland
silk holly garland
From a hardware store:
wire cutters
round-nose pliers

Cut a block of floral foam or plastic foam to fit a cast-iron or terra-cotta garden urn; cover the foam with moss. Cut a hole in the top of an acorn squash to hold a votive candle. Secure the squash to the moss-covered foam with floral picks and insert the votive candle.

In a Twinkling: Mantels

Nestle candlesticks among greenery, and rest an ornament or tree-topper finial on each candlestick, securing it with a little candle wax. Place additional ornaments along the mantel, and attach a rope of blown-glass ornaments at intervals with floral wire.

Instead of decorating with the usual apples and oranges, try vegetables and color-coordinated fruits. For a contemporary scheme, use cauliflower, cantaloupes (real and ceramic), pears, and lemons. Fill in behind the vegetables and add graceful lines that fall below the mantel's edge with foliage, such as eucalyptus, bay, or ruscus, purchased from a floral supply shop.

Give a year-round mantel display a holiday look by adding greenery and fruit or ornaments. In a traditional setting *(right),* old books nestle into garland and show off a porcelain reindeer and glass balls. In a country setting *(below),* fruit and greenery complement antique bowls and books.

more mantel ideas

■ Instead of using greenery, lay a red paisley shawl or gold piano scarf along the mantel as a background for decorations. Scrunch and gather the fabric to give it shape and create graceful swags. Hold the fabric in place with pillar candles, old Christmas books, and a silver or china tea set filled with greenery, berries, and flowers.

For brilliant color, choose red and orange sweet peppers. Arrange them to spill out of a basket or container, and balance them with candles in similar colors. Fill out the composition with pine and pinecones. A rustic snowshoe adds visual weight; you could use a toy sled instead.

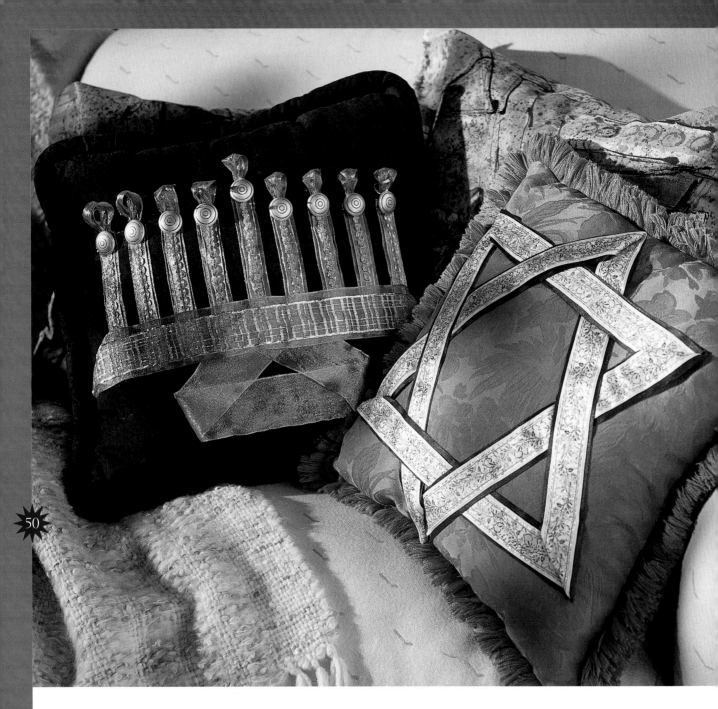

quick pillows *for* hanukkah

It's easy to make these special holiday pillows. Start with purchased pillows and add ribbon with fabric glue.

Menorah Pillow

here's how...

1 To make the menorah's main bar, cut the 2-inch-wide gold ribbon in half. Center and glue the 1½-inch-wide silver ribbon on one 18-inch length of the gold ribbon. To make the candles, center and glue the ⅝-inch-wide silver ribbon on the 1-inch-wide gold ribbon. After the glue dries, center and glue the silver braid over the silver ribbon. Cut this three-ribbon band into eight 6-inch lengths and one 7-inch length.

2 Pin the main bar to the pillow front so the top edge of the ribbon is 9 inches down from the top of the pillow. Turn under the ends at a 45-degree angle, encasing the raw edges. Mark the ribbon's position, and then remove it.

3 Center the 7-inch candle ribbon on the pillow so that the bottom of the candle is even with the bottom of the menorah's main bar. Evenly space the remaining candles on each side of the center candle, leaving ⅝ inch between them. Mark the positions of the candles and then remove them.

4 Fold the remaining wide gold ribbon into a triangle. Position it at the base of the menorah, encasing the raw edges. Mark the position and remove.

5 To make the flames, cut the copper ribbon and gold cord into nine 2-inch pieces. Fold each piece of ribbon and cord in half, and crunch the copper ribbons to give them shape. Pin the copper ribbons onto the pillow at the tops of the candles and pin the gold cords on top of the copper ribbons.

6 Pin the candles, the triangle base, and the menorah's main bar on the marked lines, enclosing or covering all raw edges of ribbons except the tops of the candles (these will be hidden by the buttons). Glue the ribbons to the pillow in this order: copper flame, gold flame, candles, triangular base, menorah's main bar. Use pins to hold the ribbons in place until the glue dries. Let one layer dry before gluing on another.

7 Erase all marking lines. Sew or glue the buttons to the top of the candles, covering the raw edges of the ribbon.

SHOPPING LIST

FOR MENORAH PILLOW:
- 17- or 18-inch square decorator pillow
- 1 yard of 2-inch-wide sheer gold ribbon
- ½ yard of 1½-inch-wide sheer silver ribbon
- 1⅜ yards of 1-inch-wide sheer gold ribbon
- 1⅜ yards of ⅝-inch-wide sheer silver ribbon
- 1⅜ yards of ⅜-inch-wide flat silver braid
- ½ yard of ¾- to 1-inch-wide copper wire-edged ribbon
- ½ yard of gold cord
- nine 1-inch-diameter silver buttons
- thread and needle or gem glue
- fabric glue
- water-soluble fabric pen or chalk pencil

Star of David Pillow

here's how...

Holding the figured ribbon on top of the blue ribbon and working with them as one, pin the ribbons to the pillow front in a triangle that fills the pillow's front. Be sure to center the top point on one edge. Miter the points of the triangle as shown *above*.

2 Make a second triangle opposite to the first, weaving the ribbons through the arms of the first triangle and pinning the ribbon to hold it in place.

3 Use thick white crafts glue to attach the figured ribbon to the blue ribbon, then glue the blue ribbon to the pillow, removing the pins as you go.

If the pillow should become soiled, spot-clean it as recommended for the fabric. Machine-washing isn't recommended.

SHOPPING LIST

FOR STAR OF DAVID PILLOW:
- 16-inch-square decorator pillow
- 3 yards of 1⅛-inch-wide figured or embroidered ribbon
- 3 yards of 1½-inch-wide blue satin ribbon
- thick white crafts glue

No space for a Christmas tree? Make a tabletop tree from a live rosemary plant or from cut greenery and flowers.

SHOPPING LIST

rosemary plant in a gallon-
    size container
pruning shears
sheet moss
heavy rubber band
½- to ¾-inch-diameter twigs
raffia
battery-operated miniature
    white Christmas lights

wee trees

Rosemary Topiary

This delightfully fragrant alternative to a conifer is the perfect size for a small apartment.

here's how...

1 Prune the rosemary plant into a cone shape.

2 Wrap sheet moss around the container, covering it from top to bottom. Hold the moss in place with a large, heavy-duty rubber band.

3 Cut twigs so they're 2 or 3 inches taller than the container. Slip the twigs under the rubber band, spacing them evenly.

4 Tie raffia tightly around the bottom of the twigs, then slip off the rubber band. Tie the twigs near the top with another piece of raffia.

5 Weave miniature Christmas lights through the rosemary branches.

52

A Temporary Tree

Bring holiday cheer to a friend with a tree-shaped arrangement.

here's how...

1 Stretch a rubber band around the pot. Slip pieces of bark under the rubber band, aligning the bottom of each piece with the bottom of the pot; the top of each piece should extend above the rim as shown. Wrap vines around the container over the rubber band; secure the ends with a twist of floral wire.

SHOPPING LIST

gallon-size plastic pot
large, heavy rubber
     band
large pieces of bark
long flexible vines
floral wire
sheet moss
floral foam
fresh evergreen cuttings
     such as juniper or pine
florist's flowers,
     holly berries, and
     variegated ivy
florist's water vials
     and florist's picks (from a
     floral supply shop)
pinecones sprayed gold

2 Tuck sheet moss between the pieces of bark. Fill the pot with floral foam, wedging one full block in the center so it extends above the rim by an amount equal to the height of the container.

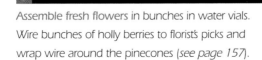

3 Assemble fresh flowers in bunches in water vials. Wire bunches of holly berries to florist's picks and wrap wire around the pinecones (*see page 157*).

53

4 Cover the sides and top of the floral foam with sheet moss. Place a 12-inch-long branch of juniper in the center of the floral foam. Insert additional shorter branches into the sides of the foam to create a cone-shaped tree. Let some of the lower branches extend below the sides of the container. Insert the ivy, holly berries, pinecones, and water vials of fresh flowers, spacing them randomly around the tree. Place the materials so they radiate out from the "trunk," following the lines of the evergreen branches.

Give your home a holiday face with outdoor decorations. Whether you opt for a simple wreath on the door or aspire to vignettes that rival Disney's, your decorations extend a merry welcome to passersby and spread a feeling of festivity throughout your neighborhood.

holiday
welcome

In addition to—or instead of— wreaths for the door (see *pages 8–11*), consider arrangements of evergreen boughs, berried branches, and pinecones for window boxes and planters. To make the ones shown here, start with plastic hanging baskets and fill them with plastic foam. For a horizontal window, like the one on *page 56*, make the arrangements alike; when you place the pots in the window box, they will blend to make a single long display. For a tall, double-hung window, like the one on *page 54*, place a few long branches asymmetrically as shown. This provides a more vertical emphasis.

From a garden center:
 four 8-inch-diameter
  plastic hanging baskets
 gravel or rocks

From a crafts store:
 2-inch-thick sheet of
  plastic foam
 hot-glue gun and glue
  sticks
 #19 floral wire
 6-inch-long floral picks

**From your yard or a
 florist:**
 birch or other long,
  slender twigs
 assorted evergreens, such
  as berried juniper,
  princess pine or
  white pine, noble
  fir, and oregonia or
  boxwood
 rose hips and winterberry
  (or other red-fruited
  branches)

56

Place gravel in the bottom of each pot for weight. Cut two pieces of plastic foam to fit each pot, trimming the top piece to fit the rim exactly. Secure the two pieces together with floral picks, then glue the plastic foam into the pot so the top of the foam is even with the rim.

Insert the birch twigs in the back of each pot for height. Next, place the tallest branches of evergreens in front of the twigs. Insert additional evergreens at the sides and front, staggering their heights so they are progressively shorter as you work toward the front of the pot.

3 Insert the winterberry branches and rose hips evenly through each arrangement for bright-red accents, positioning the branches so they repeat the lines of the evergreens.

Attach pinecones to lengths of #19 floral wire (see *page 157*) and use the wire ends as picks to secure the pinecones to the plastic foam base. After you place the pots in the window box, add greenery at each end so the branches seem to overflow the window box.

To make the planter display, follow the same procedure as for the window box arrangements, but position the birch twigs in the center of the pot rather than at the back. This keeps the design from looking flat. Place the tallest evergreens around the birch twigs and work toward the edges of the planter with progressively shorter branches. Fill in the middle of the design with greenery and add the berried branches and pinecones last.

57

◀ Decorating the chandelier lifts the eye and helps give the whole room a holiday feeling. Drape beaded garland over the fixture's arms, then hang as many glass balls as you like.

▼ Display a miniature wreath on a picture stand to give it the importance of a collector's piece.

In a Twinkling:

Embellishments

◀ For a quick, elegant centerpiece, stack footed crystal bowls on top of glass cake plates. Arrange fresh fruit, greenery, gilded nuts, and metal or papier-mâché stars in the bowls and on the plates.

◀ Pile ornaments on a glass epergne for a sparkling tabletop display.

▼ Festoon a skirted table with ribbons and bows in Christmas red and green. Use a piece of string to determine how much ribbon you'll need, holding it in place with adhesive tape. Attach the ribbon and bows to the skirt with small safety pins.

59

▲ Create a seasonal valance by layering holiday napkins over your everyday curtains. If you have a fabric-covered curtain rod, pin the folded napkins or cocktail napkins to the fabric.

What's your favorite holiday tradition?

Chances are, it involves food—legendary pies and cakes that Grandma made, golden-brown turkeys and moist stuffing, crispy latkes. We've pulled together recipes that emphasize make-ahead convenience so you'll have more time to enjoy your guests—and your favorite foods. In addition, we offer some more elaborate recipes that may become holiday traditions in their own right. And, our tips for decorating the table, serving a crowd, and getting ready for overnight guests will help you create a dazzling setting for conversation, storytelling, and laughter.

GATHERI

NG*together*

Start Christmas Day with a hearty brunch. Many of these recipes can be made ahead of time, leaving you free to enjoy your family.

morning
glories

〰 On the morning of the brunch, pop the Sausage-Cheese Strata (see *page 65*) and your choice of bread in the oven to warm while you're opening gifts. If you make Caramel-Pecan Rolls (see *page 64*), prepare them the night before, then bake them before placing the strata in the oven.

To serve the brunch, you may wish to keep place settings and dinnerware casual. Or, to enhance the feeling of celebration, bring out your best china, crystal, and silver.

Ginger Fruit Compote

1½ cups water
1 cup sugar
3 tablespoons lemon juice
2 tablespoons snipped crystallized ginger
8 cups assorted fruit (such as sliced kiwifruit, orange sections, chopped apple, sliced banana, and/or seedless red grapes)

For syrup, combine water, sugar, lemon juice, and crystallized ginger in a medium saucepan. Bring mixture to boiling; reduce heat. Cover and simmer for 5 minutes. Transfer to a bowl. Cool. Cover; chill the mixture up to 24 hours. **Place** fruit in a large serving bowl. Pour syrup over fruit, tossing gently to coat all fruit with syrup. Cover and chill up to 24 hours. Makes 12 servings.

Nutrition facts per serving: 132 cal., 0 g total fat (0 g sat. fat), 0 mg chol., 3 mg sodium, 34 g carbo., 2 g fiber, 1 g pro. Daily values: 1% vit. A, 62% vit. C, 1% calcium, 3% iron

Ginger Fruit Compote

63

Caramel-Pecan Rolls

64

To make rolls ahead, cover with oiled waxed paper, then plastic wrap. Refrigerate for 2 to 24 hours. Before baking, let the shaped rolls stand, covered, for 20 minutes at room temperature. Remove towel or wrapping. Puncture any surface bubbles with a greased toothpick.

Bake in a 375° oven, uncovered, until golden, allowing 25 to 30 minutes for unchilled rolls and 30 to 35 minutes for chilled rolls. If necessary, cover rolls with foil the last 10 minutes of baking to prevent overbrowning. Cool in pan on a wire rack for 5 minutes. Loosen edges; invert onto a serving platter. Serve warm. Makes 12 rolls.

Nutrition facts per roll: 362 cal., 15 g total fat (7 g sat. fat), 59 mg chol., 155 mg sodium, 51 g carbo., 2 g fiber, 6 g pro. Daily values: 12% vit. A, 0% vit. C, 4% calcium, 15% iron

Chocolate-Pistachio-Stuffed French Toast

Make this elegant breakfast dish ahead and freeze until the morning you need it.

- 1 1-pound unsliced loaf French bread
- 2 1- to 1½-ounce milk chocolate bars
- ⅓ cup chopped pistachio nuts
- 1½ cups graham cracker crumbs
- 8 beaten eggs
- 2 cups milk
- 1 teaspoon ground cinnamon Maple syrup or sifted powdered sugar

Cut French bread into 12 slices, each approximately 1½ inches thick. Cut a pocket in each slice of bread by starting from the bottom crust and cutting horizontally to, but not through, the top crust. Break candy bars into 12 pieces. Fill each bread pocket with 1 piece of candy and 1 rounded teaspoon of nuts.

Caramel-Pecan Rolls

Start with frozen bread dough for wonderfully rich and gooey results in a fraction of the time.

- 1¼ cups sifted powdered sugar
- ½ cup whipping cream
- ¾ cup pecan pieces
- 2 16-ounce loaves frozen sweet roll or white bread dough, thawed
- 3 tablespoons butter, melted
- ½ cup packed brown sugar
- 1 tablespoon ground cinnamon
- ¾ cup raisins (optional)

For topping, stir together powdered sugar and whipping cream in a small bowl. Pour into an ungreased 12-inch deep-dish pizza pan or a 13×9×2-inch baking pan. Sprinkle pecans evenly over mixture; set aside.

Roll each thawed loaf into a 12×8-inch rectangle on a lightly floured surface. Brush with melted butter. Stir together brown sugar and cinnamon in a small bowl; sprinkle over both rectangles. Top each with raisins, if desired. Roll up rectangles, jelly-roll style, starting from a long side. Pinch to seal. Cut each log crosswise into 6 slices. Place slices, cut side down, atop pecan mixture in pan. Cover with a towel. Let dough rise in a warm place until nearly double (about 30 minutes).

Place graham cracker crumbs in a shallow bowl. Beat together eggs, milk, and cinnamon in another shallow bowl. Dip bread into egg mixture, letting bread remain in egg mixture about 15 seconds on each side. Then dip bread into the graham cracker crumbs, turning to lightly coat the other side of the bread. Place coated slice on a greased baking sheet. Repeat dipping remaining stuffed bread into egg mixture and graham cracker crumbs.

Bake in a 450° oven about 6 minutes or until golden brown. Turn slices over and bake for 5 minutes more. Serve warm stuffed toast topped with maple syrup or powdered sugar. (To make ahead, place the baked slices in a freezer container; seal, label, and freeze up to 1 month. To serve, place the frozen stuffed bread slices in a single layer on an ungreased baking sheet. Heat, uncovered, in a 400° oven for 15 minutes or until the slices are hot.) Makes 12 slices.

Nutrition facts per slice: 268 cal., 9 g total fat (3 g sat. fat), 145 mg chol., 355 mg sodium, 34 g carbo., 1 g fiber, 11 g pro. Daily values: 9% vit. A, 1% vit. C, 9% calcium, 15% iron

Sausage-Cheese Strata

- 10 cups French bread cubes (½- to ¾-inch cubes)
- 12 ounces cooked smoked sausage links, cut into ¾-inch pieces
- 1 4-ounce can sliced mushrooms, drained
- 1 cup chopped green sweet pepper
- 6 ounces shredded sharp cheddar cheese (1½ cups)
- 4 ounces shredded Monterey Jack cheese (1 cup)
- 7 beaten eggs
- 3½ cups milk

- 2 tablespoons snipped chives
- 1 tablespoon snipped fresh oregano or 1 teaspoon dried oregano, crushed
- ½ teaspoon salt
- ¼ teaspoon pepper

Divide half of the bread cubes between 2 greased 2-quart rectangular baking dishes. Top with sausage, mushrooms, and sweet pepper. Sprinkle with cheeses. Place remaining bread cubes on top.

Combine eggs, milk, chives, oregano, salt, and pepper in a large mixing bowl. Pour half of the mixture over bread mixture in each baking dish. Cover and refrigerate for 2 to 24 hours.

Bake in a 325° oven, uncovered, for 40 to 45 minutes or until a knife inserted near centers comes out clean. Let stand 10 minutes before serving. Makes 12 servings.

Nutrition facts per serving: 378 cal., 22 g total fat (10 g sat. fat), 172 mg chol., 966 mg sodium, 23 g carbo., 0 g fiber, 21 g pro. Daily values: 17% vit. A, 12% vit. C, 25% calcium, 12% iron

tips for brunch

- Brunch typically is served between 10 a.m. and 2 p.m. and includes breakfast and luncheon items. These might be egg dishes, breakfast meats, breads, fruit, a vegetable dish, and a beverage or two.
- Since brunch is generally an informal meal, inviting guests by phone is perfectly acceptable.
- Select recipes that can be made ahead since food preparation time is often limited before a brunch.
- When it comes to food service, set out the food buffet-style so guests can help themselves. Buffet service is a simple solution for serving more people than you can comfortably seat around your table. Remember to have seating available so guests don't have to juggle their plates and beverages.

65

Sausage-Cheese Strata;
Breakfast Buttered Potatoes
(see recipe, page 66)

Apricot Breakfast Biscuits

These sweet biscuits are light and tender, perfect for brunch or breakfast.

> 2 cups all-purpose flour
> 1 tablespoon baking powder
> ¼ teaspoon salt
> ⅓ cup butter
> ⅓ cup apricot preserves
> ½ cup milk
> Milk
> 2 teaspoons sugar
> ⅛ teaspoon ground cinnamon

Stir together flour, baking powder, and salt in a medium mixing bowl. Using a pastry blender, cut in butter until mixture resembles coarse crumbs. Make a well in the center.

Snip any large pieces of preserves. Combine ½ cup milk and the preserves in a small bowl. Add all at once to dry ingredients. Stir just until dough clings together. Turn out onto a lightly floured surface. Quickly knead by gently folding and pressing dough 10 to 12 strokes or until nearly smooth.

Lightly roll or pat until ½ inch thick. Cut with a floured 2½-inch biscuit cutter, dipping cutter into flour between cuts. Place biscuits 1 inch apart on an ungreased baking sheet. Brush tops with milk. Combine sugar and cinnamon in a small bowl. Sprinkle over biscuits.

Bake in a 450° oven for 7 to 10 minutes or until golden brown. Serve warm. (To make ahead, cool completely and place biscuits in freezer containers or bags. To reheat for serving, wrap frozen biscuits in foil;

heat in a 325° oven about 20 minutes or until hot.) Makes 10 biscuits.

Nutrition facts per biscuit: 177 cal., 7 g total fat (4 g sat. fat), 17 mg chol., 233 mg sodium, 27 g carbo., 1 g fiber, 3 g pro. Daily values: 6% vit. A, 0% vit. C, 10% calcium, 9% iron

Country Scones

> ½ cup dried currants
> 2 cups all-purpose flour
> 3 tablespoons brown sugar
> 2 teaspoons baking powder
> ½ teaspoon baking soda
> ½ teaspoon salt
> ⅓ cup butter
> 1 8-ounce carton dairy sour cream
> 1 beaten egg yolk
> 1 slightly beaten egg white
> 1 tablespoon water
> 1 tablespoon coarse sugar

Place currants in a bowl and pour enough hot water over currants to cover. Let stand 5 minutes; drain well.

Stir together flour, brown sugar, baking powder, baking soda, and salt in a large mixing bowl. Using a pastry blender, cut in butter until mixture resembles coarse crumbs. Add drained currants; toss until mixed. Make a well in the center.

Combine sour cream and egg yolk in a small bowl. Add all at once to dry ingredients. Using a fork, stir just until moistened. Turn out onto a lightly floured surface. Quickly knead by gently folding and pressing dough 10 to 12 strokes or until nearly smooth.

Divide dough in half. Lightly roll or pat each half into a 6-inch circle about ½ inch thick. Cut each circle into 6 wedges. Brush tops with a mixture of egg white and 1 tablespoon water. Sprinkle with coarse sugar. Place 1 inch apart on an ungreased baking sheet.

Bake in a 425° oven for 12 to 15 minutes or until lightly browned. Cool on a wire rack for 10 minutes and serve warm. (To make ahead, cool completely and place scones in freezer containers or bags. To reheat for serving, wrap frozen scones in foil and heat in a 325° oven for 25 to 30 minutes or until heated through.) Makes 12 scones.

Nutrition facts per scone: 193 cal., 10 g total fat (6 g sat. fat), 40 mg chol., 270 mg sodium, 24 g carbo., 1 g fiber, 3 g pro. Daily values: 11% vit. A, 0% vit. C, 7% calcium, 8% iron

Breakfast Buttered Potatoes

Serve these herbed potatoes with the Sausage-Cheese Strata on page 65.

> 12 small red potatoes (about 3 pounds)
> ¼ cup butter or margarine
> 1 tablespoon snipped fresh rosemary or 1 teaspoon dried rosemary, crushed (optional)
> ½ teaspoon salt
> ¼ teaspoon pepper

Scrub potatoes thoroughly with a stiff brush. Cut potatoes into quarters. Cook potatoes in a 4-quart Dutch oven in a small amount of boiling, lightly salted water for 15 to 20 minutes or until tender; drain.

Meanwhile, heat butter or margarine in a small skillet over low heat until melted. Stir in the rosemary, if using, salt, and pepper. If using rosemary, cook and stir over low heat for 2 minutes. Gently toss cooked potatoes in a bowl with the butter mixture until potatoes are coated. Makes 12 servings.

Nutrition facts per serving: 143 cal., 4 g total fat (2 g sat. fat), 10 mg chol., 136 mg sodium, 25 g carbo., 1 g fiber, 3 g pro. Daily values: 3% vit. A, 24% vit. C, 1% calcium, 12% iron

66

Apricot Breakfast Biscuits

67

Country Scones

Hot Buttered Cider

Strudel Sticks

Strudel Sticks

2 3-ounce packages cream
cheese, softened
⅓ cup granulated sugar
2 teaspoons finely shredded
lemon peel
1 17¼-ounce package
(2 sheets) frozen puff
pastry, thawed
2 to 3 tablespoons chopped,
sliced almonds
1 tablespoon coarse sugar

For filling, combine cream cheese,
granulated sugar, and lemon peel in a
small mixing bowl; set aside.

Unfold puff pastry sheets on a lightly
floured surface. Cut each sheet into six
5×3-inch rectangles. Spread about
1 tablespoon cheese filling over each
rectangle to ½ inch from edges. Roll up
jelly-roll style, starting from one long
side. Moisten edge of dough and pinch
edges to seal. Place pastry sticks, seam
sides down, on a lightly greased baking
sheet. Make 3 or 4 diagonal cuts in top
of each pastry. Lightly brush with water.
Sprinkle with almonds and sugar.

Bake in a 350° oven for 30 to
35 minutes or until golden brown.
Serve warm or cool. (To make ahead,
cool completely and place in freezer
containers or bags. To reheat for
serving, wrap in foil and heat in a
325° oven for 15 to 20 minutes or until
heated through.) Makes 12 pastries.

Nutrition facts per pastry: 262 cal., 18 g total fat
(3 g sat. fat), 16 mg chol., 196 mg sodium,
22 g carbo., 0 g fiber, 3 g pro. Daily values:
6% vit. A, 0% vit. C, 1% calcium, 1% iron

Hot Buttered Cider

*To make a hot buttered rum drink to
enjoy later in the day, add ½ cup rum to
this recipe.*

8 cups apple cider or apple juice
2 tablespoons brown sugar
4 inches stick cinnamon
1 teaspoon whole allspice
1 teaspoon whole cloves
Peel from 1 lemon, cut into
strips
2 tablespoons butter
Cinnamon sticks (optional)

Combine cider and brown sugar in a
large saucepan. For a spice bag, tie
cinnamon, allspice, cloves, and lemon
peel in a 6-inch square of 100% cotton
cheesecloth. Add spice bag to cider
mixture. Bring to boiling over medium-
high heat; reduce heat. Cover and
simmer for 15 minutes. Remove and
discard spice bag.

Top each serving with ½ teaspoon
butter and serve with a cinnamon stick
stirrer, if desired. (To make ahead, after
discarding spice bag, chill cider and
reheat to serve. Or, keep prepared cider
warm in a crockery cooker on low-heat
setting.) Makes 10 to 12 servings.

Nutrition facts per serving: 128 cal., 2 g total fat
(1 g sat. fat), 6 mg chol., 30 mg sodium,
30 g carbo., 0 g fiber, 0 g pro. Daily values:
2% vit. A, 3% vit. C, 1% calcium, 6% iron

69

You can never have too many Christmas cookies. They're perfect for giving to friends, sharing with co-workers, or sending to school with your children.

cookies *to* share

Gingered Apricot-Raisin Drops

⅔ cup snipped dried apricots
⅔ cup golden raisins
½ cup apricot nectar
1½ teaspoons grated gingerroot or
    ¼ teaspoon ground ginger
2¼ cups all-purpose flour
1 teaspoon baking powder
¼ teaspoon salt
½ cup butter
1 cup granulated sugar
1 egg
1 teaspoon vanilla
1¼ cups chopped walnuts
    Sifted powdered sugar
    (optional)

Stir together apricots, raisins, apricot nectar, and gingerroot, if using, in a small mixing bowl. Let mixture stand for 15 minutes to plump fruit.

Stir together flour, baking powder, ground ginger, if using, and salt in a medium bowl. Beat butter in a large mixing bowl with an electric mixer on medium to high speed about 30 seconds or until softened. Add the granulated sugar and beat until fluffy. Beat in the egg and vanilla. Using a wooden spoon, stir in the fruit mixture. Stir in flour mixture until combined. Stir in walnuts. Drop dough by rounded teaspoons 2 inches apart onto a greased cookie sheet.

Bake in a 350° oven for 10 to 12 minutes or until edges are lightly browned. Transfer cookies to a wire rack and cool. If desired, sift powdered sugar over tops of cooled cookies. Makes about 60 cookies.

Nutrition facts per cookie: 70 cal., 3 g total fat (1 g sat. fat), 8 mg chol., 32 mg sodium, 10 g carbo., 0 g fiber, 1 g pro. Daily values: 2% vit. A, 1% vit. C, 0% calcium, 2% iron

Packaging instructions: Use 5-minute epoxy to attach a plastic treetop finial to the center of a glass plate. Arrange cookies around the finial, then center the plate on a large square of clear cellophane. Tie the cellophane with ribbon just below the top of the finial.

Pistachio-Almond Tarts
(see recipe, page 75)

71

Jolly Jingle Santas
(see recipe, page 72)

Gingered Apricot-Raisin Drops

Jolly Jingle Santas

Use a bell-shaped cookie cutter to make a smiling Santa, complete with a hat and beard (see photo, page 71).

1½ cups all-purpose flour
1 cup whole wheat flour
1 teaspoon baking soda
½ teaspoon ground cinnamon
¼ teaspoon salt
¼ teaspoon ground allspice
½ cup butter
½ cup packed brown sugar
1 egg
⅓ cup honey
1 teaspoon vanilla
Creamy Vanilla Frosting

72

Stir together all-purpose flour, whole wheat flour, baking soda, cinnamon, salt, and allspice in a medium bowl.

Beat butter in a large mixing bowl with an electric mixer on medium to high speed about 30 seconds or until softened. Add brown sugar and beat until fluffy. Beat in egg, honey, and vanilla until combined. Beat in as much of the flour mixture as you can with the mixer. Using a wooden spoon, stir in any remaining flour mixture. Divide dough in half. Wrap in plastic wrap. Chill dough for 2 to 24 hours.

Remove one of the portions at a time from the refrigerator; unwrap. Roll dough ¼ inch thick on a lightly floured surface. Using a 2½- to 3-inch bell-shaped cookie cutter, cut dough into bells. Place cookies 2 inches apart on an ungreased cookie sheet.

Bake in a 375° oven for 6 to 7 minutes or until edges are light brown. Transfer cookies to a rack; cool.

To decorate, use a decorating bag fitted with a medium star tip and fill it with white frosting; pipe on the brim of the hat about one-third of the way down on the cookie. Using a decorating bag fitted with a small star tip and filled with red frosting, pipe on the hat. Next, pipe on a mustache, beard, and a pom-pom on top of the hat with the white frosting. Using a decorating bag fitted with a small round tip and filled with black frosting, pipe on the eyes and mouth. If desired, miniature semisweet chocolate pieces can be used for the eyes and mouth instead of the black frosting; attach them to the cookie with a dot of icing. Makes about 42 cookies.

CREAMY VANILLA FROSTING: Beat ½ cup butter, ½ cup shortening, and 2 teaspoons vanilla in a large mixing bowl with an electric mixer on medium speed for 30 seconds. Slowly add 2 cups sifted powdered sugar, beating well. Add 2 tablespoons milk. Gradually beat in 2½ cups sifted powdered sugar and enough milk (about 1 tablespoon) to make a frosting that's easy to pipe. (For Jolly Jingle Santas, divide frosting, leaving the largest portion white, a smaller portion colored with red food coloring, and the smallest portion colored with black food coloring.)

Nutrition facts per cookie: 145 cal., 7 g total fat (3 g sat. fat), 17 mg chol., 90 mg sodium, 20 g carbo., 0 g fiber, 1 g pro. Daily values: 4% vit. A, 0% vit. C, 0% calcium, 2% iron

Chocolate-Topped Peppermint Rounds

1 cup butter
1 cup sugar
1½ teaspoons baking powder
1 egg
¼ teaspoon peppermint extract

2½ cups all-purpose flour
Small amount of red paste food coloring
66 milk chocolate stars
Vanilla Icing

Beat butter in a large mixing bowl with an electric mixer on medium to high speed about 30 seconds or until softened. Beat in the sugar and baking powder. Beat in the egg and peppermint extract. Beat in as much of the flour as you can with the mixer. Using a wooden spoon, stir in any remaining flour. Divide dough in half; tint with food coloring. Shape dough into two 9-inch-long rolls, about 1½ inches in diameter. Wrap rolls in plastic wrap. Chill for 2 to 24 hours.

Remove one of the rolls at a time from the refrigerator; unwrap. Using a sharp knife, carefully cut into ¼-inch-thick slices. Place slices 2 inches apart on an ungreased cookie sheet.

Bake in a 375° oven for 8 to 10 minutes or until edges are firm. Place a milk chocolate star in the center of each hot cookie. Cool on cookie sheet for 1 minute. Transfer cookies to a wire rack and cool. Drizzle Vanilla Icing over cooled cookies. Makes 66 cookies.

VANILLA ICING: Stir together 1 cup sifted powdered sugar, 1 teaspoon vanilla, and enough milk (2 to 4 teaspoons) in a small bowl to make an icing that is easy to drizzle. Drizzle from the tip of a spoon. Or, place the icing in a small, self-sealing plastic bag. Using scissors, snip a tiny corner from the bag and pipe icing over cookies.

Nutrition facts per cookie: 79 cal., 4 g total fat (2 g sat. fat), 11 mg chol., 41 mg sodium, 10 g carbo., 0 g fiber, 1 g pro. Daily values: 3% vit. A, 0% vit. C, 1% calcium, 1% iron

Lemon and Macadamia Nut Twists
(see recipe, page 74)

Chocolate-Topped Peppermint Rounds

Lemon and Macadamia Nut Twists

These soft, twisted cookies are full of macadamia nuts (see photo, page 73).

2½ cups all-purpose flour
1 teaspoon baking powder
½ teaspoon baking soda
¼ teaspoon salt
½ cup butter
1 cup granulated sugar
1 egg
1 teaspoon vanilla
⅔ cup buttermilk
¾ cup ground macadamia nuts or ground almonds
2 teaspoons finely shredded lemon peel
1 egg white
1 tablespoon water
Coarse sugar, pearl sugar, and/or colored sugar

74

Stir together the flour, baking powder, baking soda, and salt in a medium bowl. Beat butter in a large mixing bowl with an electric mixer on medium to high speed about 30 seconds or until softened. Add the granulated sugar and beat until fluffy. Beat in the egg and vanilla. Alternately add flour mixture and buttermilk, beating until combined. Stir in the macadamia nuts or almonds and lemon peel. Divide dough in half. Wrap in waxed paper or plastic wrap. Chill for 4 to 24 hours.

Remove one portion of dough at a time from the refrigerator. Unwrap and roll 1 tablespoon of the dough on a lightly floured surface into a 9-inch-long rope. Carefully fold dough in half, overlapping the rope ends to make a loop. Twist ends twice. Place on an ungreased cookie sheet. Repeat with remaining dough, placing twists 2 inches apart. Beat egg white and water together in a bowl. Brush egg white mixture over cookies. Sprinkle with coarse, pearl, or colored sugar.

Bake in a 375° oven for 5 to 6 minutes or until edges are set. Transfer cookies to a wire rack and cool. Makes about 45 cookies.

Nutrition facts per cookie: 79 cal., 4 g total fat (2 g sat. fat), 10 mg chol., 61 mg sodium, 10 g carbo., 0 g fiber, 1 g pro. Daily values: 2% vit. A, 0% vit. C, 1% calcium, 2% iron

Cocoa Sandies

1 cup butter
1¼ cups sifted powdered sugar
2 teaspoons vanilla
⅓ cup unsweetened cocoa powder
¼ teaspoon salt
1⅔ cups all-purpose flour
Chocolate Glaze

Beat butter in a large mixing bowl with an electric mixer on medium speed about 30 seconds or until softened. Add powdered sugar and vanilla and beat about 3 minutes or until creamy. Add cocoa powder and salt; mix well. Beat in as much of the flour as you can with the mixer. Using a wooden spoon, stir in any remaining flour. Shape the dough into 1-inch balls or 1½×¾-inch fingers. Place on an ungreased cookie sheet.

Bake in a 325° oven about 20 minutes or until just firm. Transfer cookies to a wire rack and cool.

To glaze cookies, tilt the pan of Chocolate Glaze and dip just the top of each round cookie or half of each finger into the glaze. Place on a waxed-paper-covered rack until the glaze is set. Store cookies in a tightly covered container in a cool place with waxed paper between the layers. Makes about 36 cookies.

Chocolate Glaze: Melt 4 ounces semisweet chocolate, cut up, and 3 tablespoons butter in a small saucepan over low heat, stirring frequently. Remove from heat. Stir in 1½ cups sifted powdered sugar and 3 tablespoons hot water. Stir in additional hot water, if needed, to make an icing that is easy to drizzle.

Nutrition facts per cookie: 121 cal., 7 g total fat (4 g sat. fat), 16 mg chol., 76 mg sodium, 14 g carbo., 0 g fiber, 1 g pro. Daily values: 5% vit. A, 0% vit. C, 1% calcium, 3% iron

Muddy Fudge Brownies

½ cup butter
3 ounces unsweetened chocolate
1 cup granulated sugar
2 eggs
1 teaspoon vanilla
⅔ cup all-purpose flour
¼ teaspoon baking soda
1 teaspoon instant coffee crystals
1 tablespoon whipping cream
1 cup sifted powdered sugar
2 tablespoons butter, softened
Chocolate Frosting

Melt the ½ cup butter and unsweetened chocolate in a medium saucepan over low heat, stirring constantly. Remove from heat; cool slightly. Stir in granulated sugar. Add eggs, one at a time, beating with a wooden spoon just until combined. Stir in vanilla.

Stir together flour and baking soda in a small bowl. Add flour mixture to chocolate mixture and stir just until combined. Spread batter in a greased 8×8×2-inch baking pan. Bake in a 350° oven for 30 minutes.

Meanwhile, for topping, dissolve the coffee crystals in the whipping cream. Beat together the powdered sugar and 2 tablespoons butter in a small mixing bowl with an electric mixer on medium speed. Add the whipping cream-coffee mixture and beat until creamy. Spread over the warm brownies. Chill about 1 hour or until topping is set. Carefully spread Chocolate Frosting over brownies. Chill until frosting is set. Cut the brownies into triangles or squares. Makes 16 brownies.

CHOCOLATE FROSTING: Combine 1 cup semisweet chocolate pieces and ⅓ cup whipping cream in a small saucepan. Stir over low heat until chocolate is melted and mixture begins to thicken.

Nutrition facts per brownie: 259 cal., 16 g total fat (7 g sat. fat), 54 mg chol., 103 mg sodium, 31 g carbo., 0 g fiber, 3 g pro. Daily values: 10% vit. A, 0% vit. C, 1% calcium, 6% iron

Cranberry-Pecan Bars

For easier cutting, line the baking pan with foil before adding the crust ingredients. After baking, let the bars cool slightly, then lift the foil lining out of the pan and cut the cookies into bars.

- 1 cup all-purpose flour
- 2 tablespoons sugar
- ⅓ cup butter
- ½ cup finely chopped pecans
- 1¼ cups sugar
- 2 tablespoons all-purpose flour
- 2 beaten eggs
- 2 tablespoons milk
- 1 tablespoon finely shredded orange peel
- 1 teaspoon vanilla
- 1 cup chopped cranberries
- ½ cup shredded coconut
- ½ cup finely chopped pecans

For crust, combine the 1 cup flour and the 2 tablespoons sugar in a medium mixing bowl. Using a pastry blender, cut in the butter until mixture resembles coarse crumbs. Stir in the ½ cup pecans. Press mixture into the bottom of an ungreased 13×9×2-inch baking pan. Bake in a 350° oven for 15 minutes.

Meanwhile, combine the 1¼ cups sugar and the 2 tablespoons flour in a large bowl. Stir in eggs, milk, orange peel, and vanilla. Fold in the cranberries, coconut, and the ½ cup pecans. Spread over baked crust.

Bake in a 350° oven for 30 to 35 minutes more or until top is lightly browned. Cool in pan on a wire rack. While still warm, cut into bars. Cool completely. Makes 36 bars.

Nutrition facts per bar: 89 cal., 4 g total fat (2 g sat. fat), 16 mg chol., 22 mg sodium, 12 g carbo., 0 g fiber, 1 g pro. Daily values: 2% vit. A, 1% vit. C, 0% calcium, 2% iron

Pistachio-Almond Tarts

To make the tiny tarts, just press balls of cookie dough into muffin cups, then fill, bake, and decorate (see photo, page 71).

- ½ cup butter
- 1 3-ounce package cream cheese
- 1 cup all-purpose flour
- 1 egg
- ½ cup sugar
- ½ of an 8-ounce can (½ cup) almond paste, crumbled
- ¼ cup coarsely chopped pistachios or almonds
  Chocolate Decorating Frosting
  Pistachios or almonds

For crust, beat butter and cream cheese in a medium mixing bowl with an electric mixer on medium to high

speed for 30 seconds. Stir in flour until combined. Cover and chill 1 hour or until the dough is easy to handle.

Form chilled dough into a ball; divide into 24 equal portions. Roll each portion into a ball. Press each ball evenly against the bottom and up the sides of an ungreased 1¾-inch muffin cup. Cover and set aside.

For filling, beat egg, sugar, and almond paste in a small mixing bowl until almost smooth. Stir in coarsely chopped pistachios or almonds. Fill each dough-lined muffin cup with a rounded teaspoon of filling.

Bake in a 325° oven for 25 to 30 minutes or until tops are lightly browned. Cool slightly in pans. Remove tarts from pans and cool completely on wire racks. At serving time, pipe Chocolate Decorating Frosting on top of each tart and top with a pistachio or almond. Makes 24 tarts.

CHOCOLATE DECORATING FROSTING: Beat 3 tablespoons shortening and ½ teaspoon vanilla in a small mixing bowl with an electric mixer on medium speed for 30 seconds. Add ½ cup sifted powdered sugar and 3 tablespoons unsweetened cocoa powder. Beat well. Add 2 teaspoons milk. Gradually beat in ½ cup sifted powdered sugar and enough additional milk to make a frosting of piping consistency.

Nutrition facts per tart: 145 cal., 9 g total fat (4 g sat. fat), 23 mg chol., 53 mg sodium, 15 g carbo., 0 g fiber, 2 g pro. Daily values: 5% vit. A, 0% vit. C, 2% calcium, 4% iron

75

Much of our holiday celebrating takes place around the table in the congenial atmosphere of a shared meal. It's a natural spot for decorations that promote a festive mood throughout the holidays.

festive tables

The tables here and on the following pages reflect the casual approach that suits the way we live today. Instead of a large formal flower arrangement, make several small arrangements or topiaries and display them along the table. For an even easier—and more personal—approach, assemble a collection of favorite things and group them as a centerpiece. Use party favors and place cards as decorations that guests can take home.

Pyramids of Pears

Once you've made the mossy bases for these conical topiaries, you can reuse them every year. Limes, lemons, and pears bring a new look to the classic form.

here's how...

1 Glue the floral foam into the pot, using the hot-glue gun. Fill in around the large block with small pieces. Push the dowel through the center of the foam. Or, you can fill the pot with plaster of Paris instead, and insert a dowel (see *page 19*). Glue sheet moss to the sides of the pot and over the top edges with the hot-glue gun.

2 Cover one section of the plastic foam cone with thick white crafts glue and press moss into the glue. Repeat to cover the entire cone with moss. Use floral pins to hold the moss in place until the glue dries, then remove the pins. Push the cone onto the dowel.

Open out the floral pins until they are almost L-shaped. Starting about 1 inch down from the pear's stem, slide one leg of the L down into the pear. Insert the other leg of the L into the cone near the bottom so the pear rests on the moss-covered floral foam. Continue adding pears in rows around the cone, working toward the tip. If the pear twists out of place, use a second pin or a toothpick to stabilize it.

SHOPPING LIST

assorted greenery, such
as pine, fir, and
berried juniper
silver candles
pinecones
lead-free solid silver solder
(from a hardware store)
small red and white roses
From a crafts store:
plastic foam
gold artificial berries on
wired stems
6-inch-diameter
grapevine wreath,
disassembled and cu
into 7- to 20-inch-lon
pieces
gold spray paint
cardboard and corks
pan-melt hot glue

Christmas Colors

Assemble several of these small arrangements to fill the center of
your table. They're all made on small blocks of plastic foam. Glue
some to inexpensive glass plates and insert
others into candlesticks to create a variety of heights.

here's how...

1 For each candlestick arrangement,
cut the plastic foam into a 1×2×2-inch
block. Cut a 2-inch cardboard square
and glue it to the bottom of the plastic
foam block with pan-melt hot glue (see
page 156). To secure the arrangement in
a candlestick, glue a cork to the center of
the cardboard. Or, you may prefer to
make the arrangement, then glue the
cork to the cardboard.

2 Push the candle into the
center of the plastic foam, and
secure it with hot glue. Spray
the grapevine pieces gold, then
insert them into opposite sides
of the plastic foam to establish
the arrangement's horizontal
lines. Shape the longest pieces
into half-circles that frame the
candle (but keep the vines clear
of the candle's flame). Glue
clusters of pinecones to each
side of the plastic foam.

3 Cut the greenery into sprigs 3 to 4 inches long. Insert the sprigs into the sides, top, and edges of the plastic foam block to form a mounded dome of greenery. Angle some of the side pieces down toward the tabletop.

4 Cut the silver solder into pieces of varying lengths and curl them into spirals. Insert three silver spirals into each arrangement, spacing them evenly around the sides. Insert the gold berries into the corners and top of the arrangement to accent and balance the grapevine.

5 Cut the stems of the roses 2 to 3 inches long, and tuck or glue the roses into the greenery. The roses and evergreens will dry in place. After the holidays, discard the greenery and save the roses to display in a bowl.

6 Make the two-candle arrangement in the same way, but instead of gluing the plastic foam to a cardboard square, use pan-melt hot glue to secure it to the center of a 7-inch-diameter glass plate. Glue a second small square of plastic foam to one side of the center square to hold the second candle.

here's how...

1 To make the chair-back wreaths, start with a purchased 6-inch-diameter grapevine wreath. Spray the wreath gold. Cut a 40-inch-long piece of solid silver solder (available from a hardware store). Fold the solder in half and coil about 14 inches of each end into a flat spiral (see the chair front in the photo on *page 80*). Bend the folded center of the solder upward so it forms a hook that fits the inside curve of the wreath. Wire the hook to the back of the wreath with brass wire. Shape the remaining uncoiled portion to fit over the chair back.

2 To decorate the wreath, wrap lengths of silver solder around the wreath and spiral the ends to make free-form curls. Glue stems of artificial gold berries into the grapevines. Glue small pinecones to the front of the wreath in three evenly spaced clusters, then glue fresh greenery and roses to the wreath. After your party, remove the fresh materials, or discard the evergreens and let the roses dry in place. Store the wreaths to use again next year.

TO DECORATE VOTIVE CANDLEHOLDERS, wrap an 18-inch-long piece of solid silver solder around each glass candleholder. Curl the ends into spirals. Use 20-gauge brass wire to secure gold-sprayed grapevine and sprigs of fresh pine and fir over the point where the silver-solder wires cross. Glue a small pinecone over the center to hide the wires.

timesaving tip

Reduce the stress of holiday meal preparation by setting the table early in the day or even the day before. A table that's already set when family and friends arrive sends an inviting and welcoming message and heightens the mood of celebration.

Turn chairs into thrones with swags of preserved foliage and freeze-dried flowers. You'll find most of the materials at a crafts store or floral supply shop; you may need to ask your florist to order branches of bay leaves for you. Here's how to make one swag.

For Gala Gatherings

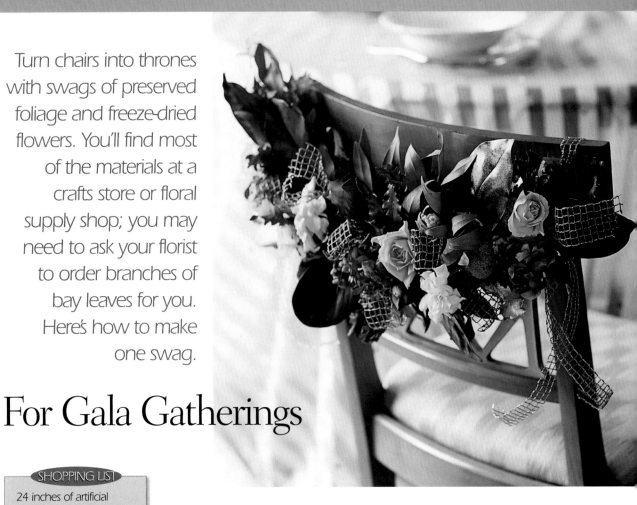

SHOPPING LIST

- 24 inches of artificial pine garland
- ¼ bunch of fresh or dried bay leaves
- ¼ bunch of preserved miniature oak leaves
- 6 magnolia leaves, lightly sprayed gold
- 4 freeze-dried roses
- 2 freeze-dried gardenias
- 2 or 3 dried hydrangea heads
- 3 yards of ribbon
- wire cutters
- floral wire
- hot-glue gun and glue sticks
- short floral picks (optional)

here's how...

1 Glue branchlets of bay leaves and oak leaves into the artificial garland. Start at the center and work toward the ends.

2 Glue the magnolia leaves, roses, gardenias, and hydrangeas into the garland, distributing each type of material evenly along the garland.

3 Cut the ribbon into 1-yard pieces. Weave one piece through the garland, securing it at intervals with wire or short floral picks. Use the remaining 1-yard pieces to tie the swag to the back of the chair.

Kwanza

African-Americans observe Kwanza from December 26 to January 1, celebrating their heritage and focusing on principles that nurture a sense of identity, community, and self-esteem.

Kwanza is a Swahili word that means "the first," referring to the first fruits of the harvest. To emphasize the harvest theme, some people like to use whatever is available at the market for the centerpiece, while others prefer to highlight tropical foodstuffs, such as mangoes, papaya, and plantains.

Other symbolic elements to include in the centerpiece are:

Mkeka, a straw mat representing tradition as the foundation on which everything else rests;

Kinara, a seven-branched candleholder symbolizing the ancestors;

Mshumaa, the seven candles representing the principles that are the focus of the celebration—unity, self-determination, collective work and responsibility, cooperative economics, purpose, creativity, and faith;

Muhindi, ears of corn standing for the children (or the potential for children) and hence posterity;

Kikombe cha umoja, the Unity Cup, used for pouring a libation to honor the ancestors;

Zawadi, small gifts that reward personal achievement.

The kinara holds black, red, and green candles, which symbolize the African-American people, their bloodshed and their continuing struggle for freedom, and the land and life.

Arrange these elements as simply as you like or, for a large neighborhood or family gathering, build a more lavish display like the one shown here. Collect baskets and wooden or crockery bowls to hold the vegetables and fruits. To use fewer materials and still achieve a look of abundance, fill the baskets and bowls with crumpled newspapers, and then arrange the fruits and vegetables on top of them.

Use small pedestals or stacks of books draped with fabric to raise some items higher than others for a more interesting display. If you plan to leave the centerpiece in place throughout the holiday, choose fruits and vegetables that will stay fresh-looking without refrigeration. These include winter squash, pumpkins, gourds, apples, sweet potatoes, and Irish potatoes.

New Year's Celebration

Bring out the silver for a sparkling salute to the coming year.

🖎 Create a festive table by assembling all of the silver containers, vases, and bowls you own and filling them with bouquets of fresh flowers. Show off your silver and dinnerware with a black tablecloth, but top it with a lacy crocheted cloth, shawl, or bedspread to keep the table from looking stark.

here's how...

1 To make the napkin clip, use wire cutters to cut an 18-inch length of 9-gauge aluminum wire (available from a hardware store). Bend the wire in half to form a hairpin shape. Use needle-nose pliers to curl each end into a spiral. Slide the clip over a napkin for your party. Your guests can take the clips home to use as oversize paper clips.

2 Mark each guest's place with a favor. Purchase small picture frames in black or silver. Use hot glue or jewelry glue to attach vintage buttons to the frames. Write each guest's name on heavy white paper cut to fit the frame; slip the paper into the frame.

Pretty Paradox

*Dazzle guests with
this fire-and-ice centerpiece.*

here's how...

Center a 2-inch-diameter pillar candle
in a clean one-half-gallon cardboard milk
carton. Stuff fresh holly and rosebuds
around the candle, then fill the carton
with water, making sure the wick is well
above the edge of the carton. Freeze the
carton until the ice is solid.

To release the centerpiece from the
mold, dip the carton in warm water; peel
the paper away. Place the candle back in
the freezer until just before serving time.
Place the candle in a shallow bowl or tray
to catch the water as the ice melts, and
cluster fresh holly, roses, and baby's breath
around the candle's base.

For festive place cards and party favors, use a permanent marker to write each guest's name on a glass Christmas ball. ▶

Shop crafts stores for woven-twig wreath forms to show off your dinner plates on an autumn table. Tiny twig wreaths make inexpensive napkin rings, and terra-cotta pots of different sizes become instant candleholders when filled with sand. (First cover the drainage hole with masking tape.) ▼

◀ Give your guests a hand by tucking a napkin and flatware into a bright-red wool glove for each place setting.

In a Twinkling:
Tabletops

◀ Celebrate autumn with a line of pears marching down the table. At the center, place a winter squash that doubles as a vase—just scoop out an opening and push the stems into the vegetable's flesh.

◄ Lemons hollowed out to receive votive candles bring sharp fragrance and glowing light to the table. Cluster the lemons on a bread plate to give them more impact and tuck sprigs of greenery around them for softness.

Fill hurricane lamps with layers of assorted fruits, nuts, and ornaments for a dazzling centerpiece. Stand the lamp on a glass plate before adding the fruit. ▶

◄ String together kumquats and gold sequins using a large-eye darning needle and raffia. Tie them into a ring to make a bracelet for each napkin.

Sugar-and-Spice Almonds
(*see recipe*, page 91)

Tropical Fruit-Black Bean Salsa

Corn Bread Rounds
with Jalapeño Jelly

Turkey and Vegetable
Tortilla Rolls
(*see recipe*, page 90)

'Tis the season for parties! Make it easy on yourself. Choose from the make-ahead appetizer recipes that follow, and keep your last-minute preparations to a minimum.

party *perfect*

 If you get the buffet table ready the day before, all you'll have to do at party time is bring out the food and welcome your guests.

Tropical Fruit-Black Bean Salsa

✳

Add the kiwifruit just before serving so the salsa doesn't become too juicy.

- 1 cup canned black beans, rinsed and drained
- 1 small papaya or mango, peeled, seeded, and chopped (¾ cup)
- ½ cup finely chopped fresh pineapple or one 8-ounce can crushed pineapple (juice pack), drained
- 1 medium orange, peeled, sectioned, and finely chopped (⅓ cup)
- ¼ cup thinly sliced green onions
- ¼ cup finely chopped red sweet pepper
- 2 tablespoons snipped fresh cilantro
- 1 tablespoon lime or lemon juice
- 3 small kiwifruit, peeled and finely chopped (⅔ cup)
  Tortilla chips

Stir together black beans, papaya or mango, pineapple, orange, green onions, sweet pepper, cilantro, and lime or lemon juice in a medium mixing bowl. Cover and chill for 4 to 24 hours. Stir in kiwifruit. Transfer to serving dish using a slotted spoon. Serve with tortilla chips. Makes about 3½ cups salsa.

Nutrition facts per tablespoon (without tortilla chips): 8 cal., 0 g total fat (0 g sat. fat), 0 mg chol., 11 mg sodium, 2 g carbo., 0 g fiber, 0 g pro. Daily values: 1% vit. A, 12% vit. C, 0% calcium, 0% iron

Corn Bread Rounds With Jalapeño Jelly

To make a colorful appetizer tray, top some of the corn bread rounds with red jelly and others with green jelly.

- ¾ cup all-purpose flour
- ¼ cup cornmeal
- 1 tablespoon sugar
- 1 teaspoon baking powder
- ¼ teaspoon salt
- ¼ cup butter
- ¼ cup milk
- 2 tablespoons canned diced green chili peppers, drained
- 1 tablespoon oil-packed dried tomatoes, drained and finely chopped

- 1 8-ounce tub cream cheese
- ¼ cup red and/or green jalapeño jelly, melted

Stir together flour, cornmeal, sugar, baking powder, and salt in a medium mixing bowl. Using a pastry blender, cut in the butter until mixture resembles coarse crumbs. Add the milk, chili peppers, and tomatoes all at once and stir until the mixture forms a ball.

Turn dough out onto a lightly floured surface and knead by gently folding and pressing dough for 8 to 10 strokes. Roll the dough until ¼ inch thick. Cut with a floured 2-inch round biscuit cutter, dipping cutter into flour between cuts. Place dough rounds on an ungreased baking sheet.

Bake in a 400° oven for 12 to 15 minutes or until golden. Remove and cool on a wire rack. (To make ahead, freeze baked rounds in freezer containers. Thaw before using.) To serve, spread cream cheese atop each round. Drizzle with melted jelly. Makes about 18 rounds.

Nutrition facts per round: 109 cal., 7 g total fat (4 g sat. fat), 21 mg chol., 133 mg sodium, 10 g carbo., 0 g fiber, 2 g pro. Daily values: 8% vit. A, 2% vit. C, 3% calcium, 3% iron

Cranberry-Praline Mascarpone Spread

Cranberry-Praline Mascarpone Spread

For make-ahead convenience, you can prepare the praline mixture up to 3 days ahead and store it at room temperature. The cheese mixture also can be made ahead and stored, covered, in the refrigerator. Just before serving, stir the two together.

⅓ cup finely chopped almonds or hazelnuts (filberts)
¼ cup sugar
1 tablespoon butter
¼ teaspoon vanilla
1 8-ounce carton mascarpone cheese or one 8-ounce package cream cheese, softened
½ teaspoon finely shredded orange peel
1 tablespoon Grand Marnier or orange juice
¼ cup dried cranberries or tart red cherries, chopped
1 tablespoon milk (optional)
Orange peel curls (optional)
Assorted crisp cookies (such as Pirouettes or shortbread)
Fresh fruit (such as strawberries, apple slices, pear slices, and/or grapes)

Line a baking sheet with foil. Butter the foil and set aside.

Combine almonds or hazelnuts, sugar, butter, and vanilla in a heavy 8-inch skillet. Cook over medium heat (do not stir) until sugar begins to melt, shaking skillet occasionally. Reduce heat to low; continue cooking until sugar turns golden, stirring frequently with a wooden spoon. Immediately spread coated nuts on prepared baking sheet. Cool nuts and break into chunks; finely chop. Store in airtight container.

Beat cheese, orange peel, and Grand Marnier in a mixing bowl with an electric mixer on medium speed until combined. Stir in the dried cranberries or cherries.

Before serving, stir in finely chopped praline mixture and 1 tablespoon milk, if desired, to thin consistency of spread. Transfer to a serving bowl. If desired, garnish with orange peel curls. Serve with cookies and fruit. Makes 1½ cups.

Nutrition facts per tablespoon spread: 70 cal., 6 g total fat (3 g sat. fat), 13 mg chol., 11 mg sodium, 4 g carbo., 0 g fiber, 2 g pro. Daily values: 0% vit. A, 0% vit. C, 0% calcium, 0% iron

Turkey and Vegetable Tortilla Rolls

Vary the color of the sweet peppers, if you like (see photo, page 88).

12 asparagus spears
1 large red sweet pepper
1 8-ounce package cream cheese, softened
2 tablespoons milk
2 teaspoons snipped fresh rosemary or ½ teaspoon dried rosemary, crushed
1 to 2 teaspoons brown mustard
4 7- or 8-inch flour tortillas
2 6-ounce packages thinly sliced cooked smoked turkey
Lettuce leaves

Cook asparagus in a small amount of boiling water for 4 to 8 minutes or until crisp-tender. Drain thoroughly on paper towels. Cut pepper into strips.

Beat cream cheese, milk, rosemary, and mustard together in a mixing bowl with an electric mixer until the mixture is smooth.

To assemble, place 1 tortilla on a flat surface. Spread one-fourth of the cream cheese mixture on the tortilla. Place one-fourth of the turkey on cream cheese mixture. Arrange 3 of the asparagus spears and several pepper strips over the turkey. Roll up tortilla. Repeat with remaining tortillas and filling ingredients. Wrap each tortilla roll in plastic wrap; chill up to 12 hours. To serve, remove plastic wrap and cut each tortilla roll into 1-inch-thick slices. Place, cut side up, on a lettuce-lined plate. Makes 24 to 28 slices.

Nutrition facts per slice: 86 cal., 6 g total fat (2 g sat. fat), 11 mg chol., 205 mg sodium, 4 g carbo., 0 g fiber, 4 g pro. Daily values: 5% vit. A, 17% vit. C, 1% calcium, 3% iron

Gunpowder Guacamole

Sugar-and-Spice Almonds

To make extra nuts for gift giving, prepare a separate batch instead of doubling the recipe. The nuts clump together if cooked in larger quantities (see photo, page 88).

- ½ cup sugar
- ½ teaspoon finely shredded orange peel
- ¼ teaspoon ground cinnamon
- ⅛ teaspoon salt
- ⅛ teaspoon ground allspice
- ⅛ teaspoon ground nutmeg
- 1 cup unblanched whole almonds

Line a baking sheet with foil. Butter the foil and set aside.

Combine sugar, orange peel, cinnamon, salt, allspice, and nutmeg in a heavy 10-inch skillet. Stir in almonds. Cook over medium-high heat (do not stir) until sugar begins to melt, shaking skillet occasionally (this will take 5 to 7 minutes). Reduce heat to low; continue cooking until sugar turns golden brown, stirring frequently with a wooden spoon (this will take 2 to 4 minutes).

Immediately pour nut mixture onto the prepared baking sheet. Spread into a single layer with a wooden spoon. Cool completely. Break apart, if necessary. Store in an airtight container. Makes 2 cups.

Nutrition facts per ¼ cup serving: 124 cal., 7 g total fat (1 g sat. fat), 0 mg chol., 34 mg sodium, 15 g carbo., 1 g fiber, 4 g pro. Daily values: 0% vit. A, 0% vit. C, 4% calcium, 5% iron

Gunpowder Guacamole

- 2 medium avocados, seeded, peeled, and cut up
- 1 tablespoon lime juice
- 1 medium red sweet pepper, roasted and chopped or ½ cup chopped purchased roasted red sweet peppers
- 3 green onions, finely chopped
- 1 to 2 tablespoons chopped jalapeño or serrano chili peppers*
- ¼ teaspoon salt
- ¼ teaspoon ground black pepper
- ⅛ teaspoon ground red pepper
  Tortilla chips

Combine avocados and lime juice in a medium mixing bowl. Using a potato masher, coarsely mash avocado mixture (mixture should be slightly lumpy).

Stir roasted sweet pepper, green onions, jalapeño or serrano peppers, salt, black pepper, and red pepper into avocado mixture. Cover and chill until serving time. Serve with tortilla chips. Makes about 1⅔ cups.

***Note:** When handling hot chili peppers, avoid touching your eyes; wear disposable gloves to protect your skin.

Nutrition facts per tablespoon (without tortilla chips): 26 cal., 2 g total fat (0 g sat. fat), 0 mg chol., 21 mg sodium, 2 g carbo., 1 g fiber, 0 g pro. Daily values: 3% vit. A, 12% vit. C, 0% calcium, 1% iron

timesaving tips

■ Choose a few "star" recipes, then round out your food table with purchased items, such as trays of cheeses, meats, fresh vegetable cruidités, and fruit pieces. Accompany these with baskets of crackers, baguette slices, and chips.

■ Plan your menu and grocery list one to two weeks in advance and include some make-ahead recipes.

■ If you love to entertain but have no time to cook, consider hiring a caterer or a friend who cooks to help with the food preparations. Often a caterer will let you supply the recipes, if desired.

■ Hire someone to help pour beverages and keep food trays replenished so you can enjoy your own party.

91

Three-Cheese Loaf

PARTY PERFECT

Three-Cheese Loaf

2 cups finely shredded
     cheddar cheese (8 ounces)
1 cup finely shredded Swiss
     cheese (4 ounces)
½ of an 8-ounce package
     cream cheese
⅓ cup dairy sour cream
2 teaspoons horseradish mustard
⅛ teaspoon onion powder
⅔ cup chopped pistachio nuts,
     walnuts, or pecans
   Assorted crackers and fruits

Bring cheddar cheese, Swiss cheese, and cream cheese to room temperature. Add sour cream, horseradish mustard, and onion powder. Beat until combined and mixture is slightly fluffy.

Line one 7½×3½×2-inch or two 5¾×3×2-inch loaf pan(s) with plastic wrap. Sprinkle half the nuts in the large pan or one-fourth of the nuts in each of the smaller pans. Spread half of the cheese mixture over nut layer (one-fourth in each of the smaller pans). Top with remaining nuts; spread with remaining cheese mixture, pressing into pan(s) to make an even layer. Cover and chill at least 2 hours.

To serve, unmold onto serving plate; remove plastic wrap and let stand 10 minutes before serving. Serve with crackers and fruits. Makes 20 servings.

Nutrition facts per serving spread: 120 cal., 10 g total fat (5 g sat. fat), 25 mg chol., 109 mg sodium, 2 g carbo., 0 g fiber, 6 g pro. Daily values: 8% vit. A, 0% vit. C, 12% calcium, 2% iron

Nutty Blue Cheese Rolls

These flavorful appetizers get a head start with a refrigerated piecrust.

⅔ cup finely chopped walnuts
⅓ cup crumbled blue cheese
1 tablespoon finely snipped
     parsley
¼ teaspoon pepper
½ of a 15-ounce package (1 crust)
     folded refrigerated unbaked
     piecrust
1 tablespoon milk
2 teaspoons grated Parmesan
     cheese
   Finely snipped parsley

For filling, stir together walnuts, blue cheese, 1 tablespoon parsley, and the pepper in a medium bowl. Unfold piecrust on a lightly floured surface according to package directions. Spread filling evenly over the crust. Cut the pastry circle into 12 wedges. Starting at the wide ends, loosely roll up wedges. Place rolls, tip side down, on a greased baking sheet. (To make ahead, cover and chill rolls for up to 24 hours.)

Brush rolls lightly with milk before baking. Sprinkle with Parmesan cheese and additional parsley.

Bake in a 425° oven about 15 minutes or until golden. Cool slightly on a wire rack. Serve warm. Makes 12 rolls.

Nutrition facts per roll: 139 cal., 10 g total fat (1 g sat. fat), 8 mg chol., 130 mg sodium, 9 g carbo., 3 g fiber, 3 g pro. Daily values: 1% vit. A, 1% vit. C, 2% calcium, 1% iron

Nutty Blue Cheese Rolls

If you have more people than you have places around the dining table, don't cut back on your guest list. Just tackle the seating—and serving—situation with a little creativity.

serving *a* crowd

∾ The easiest way to feed a crowd is to let people serve themselves from a buffet. If you don't have a large enough dining table—or if you want to keep traffic moving smoothly by setting out food in several rooms—make a temporary table. Lay a sheet of plywood or an old door over a pair of sawhorses and drape sheets, coverlets, quilts, or tablecloths over the construction to dress it up for the occasion.

When it comes to seating, be sure to provide plenty of low tables beside chairs and sofas where guests can place their drinks. If you prefer to have everyone seated around tables, look first to living room tables that ordinarily display lamps, books, and bibelots.

Move the table out into the room, add a washable overskirt for a cloth, and draw up armchairs, parsons chairs, or folding director's chairs.

If you still need more tables and chairs—or serving pieces, dinnerware, or table linens—consider renting them. Rental companies specializing in all kinds of party goods, table linens, and dinnerware are cropping up across the country, and the cost can be surprisingly reasonable. You needn't settle for boring card tables and folding chairs, either. Party rental businesses can provide an assortment of cloths and skirts to dress up tables and coordinating slipcovers for the chairs. Renting linens entails a smaller out-of-pocket expense than

buying them—and when the party's over, you won't have to do the laundry.

Renting special serving pieces or extra place settings that you don't normally need is also convenient: You won't need to store them, and usually you don't have to wash them before returning them. Most party rental businesses have a showroom set up like a retail store, displaying sample stock in settings that can give you ideas of how pieces can be combined and used. Be sure to check the rental agreement for delivery charges, damage wavers, and replacement terms. Ordinary wear and tear on table linens, for example, such as food stains and candle wax, won't cost extra, but you will be charged a fee if you return linens with rips, burns, or signs of obvious misuse.

family traditions

Turn helping in the kitchen into a game. "I jot down tasks on slips of paper, then ask each person to draw a task from a jar. This allows everyone to help with dinner, including kids, dads, and even Grandpa. Plus, I get to spend more time visiting and less time in the kitchen."

— *Sharon Hagemann*
Sandpoint, Idaho

make-it-easy entertaining

■ To make sure you enjoy your own party, do as much as you can before the day of the event. Get serving dishes and platters out and arrange them on the buffet table so you'll know where everything goes. Plates, napkins, flatware, and drinking glasses can go on the table ahead of time, too.

■ If you're serving appetizers or build-your-own sandwiches, divide them in half and make double dishes. As one plate of appetizers or sandwich fixings gets picked over, simply remove it from the buffet table and replace it with the second plate.

■ Don't leave hot or cold foods out for more than two hours at room temperature. The same goes for foods that include dairy products.

■ Keep cold foods cold by putting them on ice. Use a slow cooker to keep hot foods hot. Put canned or bottled beverages in a cooler full of ice to keep from having to open the refrigerator door so often.

■ *Take a cue from this intimate breakfast for two: When you want to serve a seated dinner to more guests than your dining table will accommodate, set up skirted tables around the house. Turn a card table into a more generously sized table with a plywood round from a home-improvement center and layer fabrics over it.*

turkey *basics*

Because many of us save turkey and all the trimmings for a once- or twice-a-year feast, even experienced cooks can use a refresher course on buying, thawing, and cooking the traditional bird. Here are some tips. For recipes, see *pages 100–101.*

unstuffed* whole turkey roasting guide

Ready-to-cook turkey weight	Oven temperature	Roasting time
8 to 12 pounds	325°	2¾ to 3 hours
12 to 14 pounds	325°	3 to 3¾ hours
14 to 18 pounds	325°	3¾ to 4¼ hours
18 to 20 pounds	325°	4¼ to 4½ hours
20 to 24 pounds	325°	4½ to 5 hours

Stuffed birds generally require 15 to 45 minutes more roasting time than unstuffed birds.

buying and thawing a turkey

■ When buying a turkey, allow 1 pound per adult serving if the bird weighs 12 pounds or less. For larger turkeys, count on ¾ pound for each serving. If you want leftovers, buy a bird that's 2 to 4 pounds larger than the size you'll need for serving.

■ While not all turkeys are labeled indicating whether the bird is a hen or tom, select a "hen" turkey if you want more white meat and a "tom" if you want more dark meat. Also check for the "sell by" date on the label of a fresh turkey. This date is the last day the turkey should be sold by the retailer. The unopened turkey should maintain its quality and be safe to use for one or two days after the "sell by" date.

■ If you're buying a frozen turkey, look for packaging that is clean, undamaged, and frost free. Allow plenty of time to thaw a frozen turkey. For a whole frozen turkey, leave the bird in its wrapping and place it on a tray in the refrigerator. Plan on at least 24 hours for every 5 pounds and don't count the day you'll be roasting the bird. (Once thawed, turkeys will keep one or two days in the refrigerator.)

■ If you run short of time and the turkey isn't completely thawed the day you plan to roast it, place the bird in a clean sink full of COLD water and change the water every 30 minutes. Do NOT thaw turkey at room temperature or in warm water—these methods will allow harmful bacteria to grow quickly to dangerous levels. You'll know the bird is ready for roasting if the giblets can be removed easily and there are no ice crystals in the interior cavity. If the turkey is still frozen in the center, the bird will cook unevenly.

preparing a turkey for roasting

■ Once the turkey has thawed, release the legs from the leg clamp or the band of skin crossing the tail. Also remove the giblets and neck from cavities. Rinse the turkey inside and out, let it drain, and pat dry with paper towels.

■ If you don't have an accurate meat thermometer, cook the stuffing separately because there is no visual test for stuffing doneness. Mix the stuffing just before you stuff and roast the bird. Allow ¾ cup of stuffing per pound of bird. Spoon some stuffing loosely into the neck cavity. Pull the neck skin over the stuffing and fasten to the back with a short skewer.

■ Loosely spoon stuffing into the body cavity rather than packing it. Otherwise, it won't get hot enough by the time the turkey is cooked. Spoon any remaining stuffing into a casserole; cover and chill until ready to bake. Tuck the legs under the band of skin that crosses the tail or reset the legs into the leg clamp. Or, tie the legs with kitchen string to the tail. Twist the wing tips under the back.

■ Place the turkey, breast side up, on a rack in a shallow roasting pan. Insert a meat thermometer into the center of an inside thigh muscle so the bulb doesn't touch bone. Cover the turkey loosely with foil, leaving space between the bird and the foil. Press the foil over the drumsticks and neck. Roast in a 325° oven using the timings in the chart on *page 98* as a guide.

■ When the bird has been in the oven for two-thirds of the roasting time, cut the skin between the drumsticks but don't remove the clamp. Remove the foil the last 30 minutes to let the turkey brown.

■ When the turkey is done, the thigh meat should be 180° and the center of the stuffing should be at least 165°. (Check the temperatures with a thermometer—see tips *below*.) The drumsticks should move easily in their sockets, and their thickest parts should feel soft when pressed. In addition, juices from the thigh should run clear when it's pierced deeply with a long-tined fork. Remove the turkey from the oven and cover loosely with foil. Let stand for 20 minutes. Release the legs from the leg clamp. To avoid possible burns, don't remove the leg clamp until turkey has cooled.

■ Do not allow the turkey to remain at room temperature more than two hours after it comes out of the oven. Cooked turkey and stuffing may be refrigerated, separately, up to two days.

thermometer tips

■ Use a thermometer to ensure that the turkey and the stuffing have reached a safe temperature for consumption.

■ A meat thermometer is used for larger cuts of poultry (and meat). Insert the thermometer into the turkey at the beginning of the cooking time, making sure it doesn't touch bone or the pan.

■ An instant-read thermometer, also called a rapid-response thermometer, measures a wide range of temperatures. These thermometers are not designed to stay in food during cooking. Remove the food from the oven, then insert the thermometer into the thickest portion of the food, not touching bone or pan.

■ Check a thermometer for accuracy by submerging at least 2 inches of the stem of the thermometer in boiling water. It should read 212°F.

Roast Turkey with Bourbon-Butter Glaze

Part of the glaze is slipped under the turkey's skin and the rest is brushed over the turkey for a golden color. If the turkey is stuffed, add extra roasting time.

½ cup butter, softened
¼ cup packed brown sugar
2 tablespoons chopped fresh
    marjoram or 2 teaspoons
    dried marjoram, crushed
1 teaspoon finely shredded
    lemon peel
1 14- to 16-pound turkey
½ cup bourbon
  Salt
  Pepper

For glaze, combine butter, brown sugar, marjoram, and lemon peel in a small mixing bowl.

Rinse turkey and pat dry with paper towels. Place turkey, breast side up, on a rack in a shallow roasting pan. Using your fingers, separate turkey skin from breast meat, being careful not to tear skin or pierce meat. Spread about half of the butter mixture over the breast meat under the skin.

Melt remaining butter mixture; cool slightly. Stir in bourbon. Brush mixture over outside of turkey. Season turkey with salt and pepper. Pull neck skin to back and fasten to back with a short skewer. Tuck drumsticks under band of skin that crosses tail. If there isn't a band, tie drumsticks to tail. Twist wing tips under back.

Insert a meat thermometer into the center of one of the inside thigh muscles. The thermometer bulb should not touch the bone. Cover turkey

loosely with foil. Roast turkey in a 325° oven for 3¾ to 4¼ hours or until meat thermometer registers 180°.

When turkey is two-thirds done, cut skin or string between drumsticks. Remove foil the last 30 minutes to let bird brown. Turkey is done when drumsticks move very easily in their sockets and their thickest parts feel soft when pressed. Remove turkey from oven and cover loosely with foil. Let stand 20 minutes before carving. Makes 12 to 15 servings.

Nutrition facts per serving: 432 cal., 23 g total fat (9 g sat. fat), 174 mg chol., 231 mg sodium, 4 g carbo., 0 g fiber, 45 g pro. Daily values: 18% vit. A, 0% vit. C, 4% calcium, 22% iron

---

Rich Pan Gravy

Pour pan drippings from roast turkey into a large measuring cup. Skim and reserve fat from pan drippings. Measure fat and add melted butter or margarine, if necessary, to make ½ cup. Add chicken broth to the skimmed drippings to measure 2½ cups total; set aside.

Pour the ½ cup fat into a medium saucepan (discard any remaining fat). Stir in ½ cup all-purpose flour, ¼ teaspoon salt, and ⅛ teaspoon pepper. Cook and stir over medium heat for 2 minutes. Gradually whisk broth mixture into flour mixture. Cook and stir until thickened and bubbly. Add ½ cup milk. Cook and stir 1 minute more. Makes about 3½ cups.

Nutrition facts per 2 tablespoons: 41 cal., 3 g total fat (2 g sat. fat), 9 mg chol., 57 mg sodium, 2 g carbo., 0 g fiber, 0 g pro. Daily values: 3% vit. A, 0% vit. C, 0% calcium, 0% iron

---

Herbed Roasted Turkey

¼ cup olive oil
1 tablespoon snipped fresh basil
1 tablespoon snipped
    fresh oregano
1 tablespoon snipped fresh
    parsley
2 cloves garlic, minced
¼ teaspoon salt
1 8- to 12-pound turkey

Combine olive oil, basil, oregano, parsley, garlic, and salt in a small bowl.

Rinse turkey and pat dry with paper towels. Place turkey, breast side up, on a rack in a shallow roasting pan. Using your fingers, separate turkey skin from breast meat, being careful not to tear skin or pierce meat. Spread about half of the oil mixture over the breast meat under the skin. Brush remaining mixture over outside of turkey. Pull neck skin to back and fasten with a short skewer. Tuck drumsticks under band of skin that crosses tail. If there isn't a band, tie drumsticks to tail. Twist wing tips under back.

Insert a meat thermometer into the center of one of the inside thigh muscles. The thermometer bulb should not touch the bone. Cover turkey loosely with foil. Roast turkey in a 325° oven for 2¾ to 3 hours or until meat thermometer registers 180°.

When turkey is two-thirds done, cut skin or string between drumsticks. Remove foil the last 30 minutes to let bird brown. Turkey is done when drumsticks move very easily in their sockets and their thickest parts feel soft when pressed. Remove turkey from oven and cover loosely with foil. Let stand 20 minutes before carving. Makes 8 to 12 servings.

Nutrition facts per serving: 526 cal., 28 g total fat (7 g sat. fat), 216 mg chol., 220 mg sodium, 0 g carbo., 0 g fiber, 64 g pro. Daily values: 15% vit. A, 1% vit. C, 5% calcium, 30% iron

Spice-Rubbed Turkey

¼ cup cooking oil
1 tablespoon chili powder
1 teaspoon ground cumin
1 teaspoon garlic salt
½ teaspoon ground coriander
1 12- to 14-pound turkey

Combine cooking oil, chili powder, cumin, garlic salt, and coriander in a small bowl.

Rinse turkey and pat dry with paper towels. Place turkey, breast side up, on a rack in a shallow roasting pan. Using your fingers, separate turkey skin from breast meat, being careful not to tear skin or pierce meat. Spread about half the oil mixture over the breast meat under the skin. Brush remaining mixture over outside of turkey. Pull neck skin to back and fasten with a short skewer. Tuck drumsticks under

band of skin that crosses tail. If there isn't a band, tie drumsticks to tail. Twist wing tips under back.

Insert a meat thermometer into the center of one of the inside thigh muscles. The thermometer bulb should not touch the bone. Cover turkey loosely with foil. Roast turkey in a 325° oven for 3 to 3¾ hours or until meat thermometer registers 180°.

When turkey is two-thirds done, cut skin or string between drumsticks. Remove foil the last 30 minutes to let bird brown. Turkey is done when drumsticks move very easily in their sockets and their thickest parts feel soft when pressed. Remove turkey from oven and cover loosely with foil. Let stand 20 minutes before carving. Makes 12 to 14 servings.

Nutrition facts per serving: 315 cal., 17 g total fat (4 g sat. fat), 126 mg chol., 267 mg sodium, 1 g carbo., 0 g fiber, 37 g pro. Daily values: 11% vit. A, 0% vit. C, 3% calcium, 20% iron

Corn Bread and Dried Peach Dressing

Southern-Style Corn Bread
½ cup chopped celery with leaves
½ cup chopped onion
⅓ cup butter
1½ cups chopped cooked ham
2 beaten eggs
¼ cup snipped fresh parsley
2 teaspoons dried sage, crushed
½ teaspoon pepper
¼ teaspoon salt
1½ cups chopped dried peaches
1 cup coarsely chopped pecans, toasted
1 to 1⅓ cups chicken broth

Prepare corn bread; cut into ½-inch pieces. Place in a large shallow baking pan. Bake in a 325° oven about 15 minutes or until bread pieces are slightly dry, stirring once. Transfer to a very large bowl.

Cook celery and onion in butter in a large skillet or saucepan over medium heat about 5 minutes or until vegetables are tender. Add to corn bread in bowl. Add ham.

Combine eggs, parsley, sage, pepper, and salt in a small bowl. Add to corn bread mixture; toss lightly until mixed. Add peaches and pecans. Drizzle with enough of the broth to moisten, tossing very lightly until mixed. Use to stuff a 14- to 16-pound turkey. Spoon any remaining stuffing into a casserole; cover and chill until ready to bake. The last 45 minutes of turkey roasting, add the casserole to the oven and bake, covered, until heated through. Makes 12 to 15 servings.

SOUTHERN-STYLE CORN BREAD: Stir together 2 cups yellow cornmeal, 1 cup all-purpose flour, 4 teaspoons baking powder, and ½ teaspoon salt in a mixing bowl. Lightly beat together 1½ cups buttermilk, 2 eggs, and ⅓ cup melted butter. Add to flour mixture and stir just until batter is smooth (do not overbeat). Pour into a greased 9×9×2-inch baking pan. Bake in a 425° oven for 25 to 30 minutes or until golden brown.

Nutrition facts per serving dressing: 370 cal., 20 g total fat (8 g sat. fat), 109 mg chol., 693 mg sodium, 38 g carbo., 3 g fiber, 12 g pro. Daily values: 17% vit. A, 11% vit. C, 14% calcium, 20% iron

101

▼ Before placing a serving on a dessert plate, "stencil" the plate, using a paper doily, a sieve, and cinnamon, cocoa powder, or powdered sugar. Place the doily on a plate and spray lightly with nonstick spray coating. Sift a topping over the stencil, then lift off the doily carefully. Stencil the dessert in the same way (omit the spray coating). Use cinnamon, unsweetened cocoa powder, or cinnamon-sugar mixture on cake with a light-colored frosting. Try powdered sugar on a chocolate-frosted cake.

▲ Decorate a pie, frosted cake, or cookie platter with chocolate stars. Spoon melted and cooled chocolate into a small, self-sealing plastic bag. Snip off one corner of the bag, and pipe the melted chocolate onto a waxed-paper-lined baking sheet, forming a square. Pipe a second square at a 45-degree angle to the first. Let chocolate stand until firm.

In a Twinkling:
Treats

102

◄ Freeze cranberries and use them instead of ice to cool the champagne. As the berries thaw, they take on a frosty charm.

For Sugared Cranberries, combine 2 tablespoons water and 1 tablespoon refrigerated egg product. Brush cranberries with the mixture, then roll in granulated sugar. Use within 2 hours to decorate desserts.

◀ For a simple but festive presentation, arrange loops of wired star garland in random curls around the base of a pedestal cake plate.

▲ To make small chocolate curls, draw a vegetable peeler across a bar of milk chocolate. The chocolate curls best if it is at room temperature. Use the narrow side of the chocolate bar for narrow curls and the broad surface for wide curls.

To make a miniature herb bouquet for decorating a serving plate or topping an appetizer tart, select three or four kinds of herbs with different textures and colors. Cut the stems about 4 inches long and arrange herbs to show off the different types before tying with a string. If you like, you can dye the string with tea.

▼

▲ Give your desserts a sophisticated look by pooling the sauce under the dessert instead of over it. Spoon 1 or 2 tablespoons of sauce on each dessert plate and tilt the plate to spread the sauce evenly. If you like, pipe a contrasting colored sauce to outline the edge, using a pastry bag with a round tip.

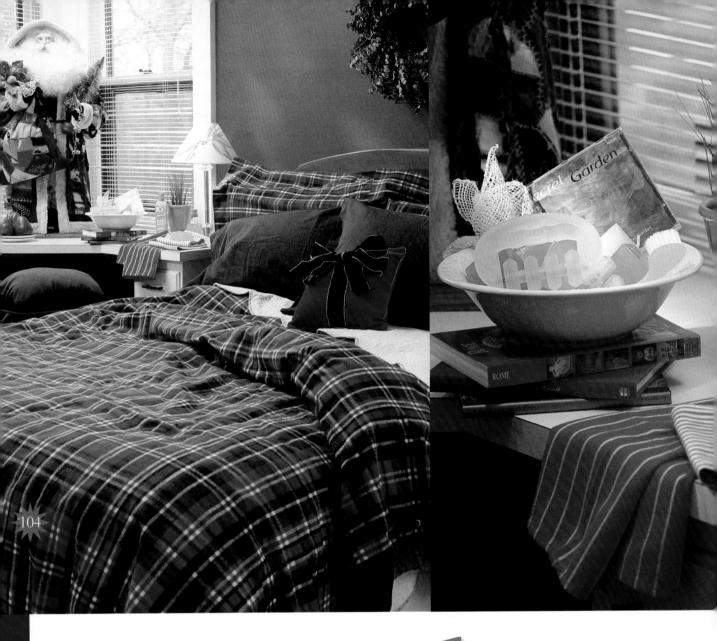

room *in the* inn

When the family heads to *your* home for the holidays,
set the stage for a happy gathering with festive touches in the
guest room. Your attention to details will make their stay a
memorable one.

Guest Room Makeover

Give the guest room a holiday face with Christmas-colored bed linens and a few decorations.

dress the bed for the season with a duvet made from red-and-green plaid flannel sheets (for instructions on stitched and no-sew versions, see *page 106*). Add plump pillows in coordinating shams and cases, and toss in a small decorator pillow wrapped with velvet ribbon.

make room for guests' belongings by clearing the dresser top and a drawer or two, and make space available in the closet, along with hangers for skirts and pants.

provide a bedside reading lamp and a basket of magazines and books. An alarm clock, tissues, a carafe of water, and a drinking glass are also considerate and practical gestures.

if you don't have the luxury of a separate bath for guests, set out an array of scented soaps, bath oils, lotions, and fluffy towels in the bedroom so your visitors will know they're welcome to indulge themselves.

for late-night snacking, leave a tray of treats in the room (see *pages 108–109* for recipes). It's also thoughtful to get the coffeemaker set up and ready to go so guests can make a pot if they're up first in the morning.

Holiday Duvet Covers

Start with queen-size flat flannel sheets to make this cover for a double-bed comforter or duvet.

SHOPPING LIST

one queen-size plaid flat flannel sheet and one in spruce green (see *page 158* for a mail-order source)
For no-sew version:
  65 grommets ½ inch in diameter
  grommet tool
  heavy chenille yarn
  two ½-inch-diameter wooden beads
For stitched version:
  thread to match fabrics
  heavy-duty snaps
  star-shaped novelty buttons

here's how...

no-sew version

1 Trim 21 inches from the bottom edge of the green sheet; press under a 3-inch hem on the bottom and side edges of both sheets. Place the sheets with wrong sides facing and the green sheet on top, aligning the bottom and side edges. The plaid sheet will extend beyond the green sheet by 24 inches to make the top flap.

2 At each top corner of the plaid sheet, attach a grommet about 1 inch in from the side and top edges. Fold the flap down over the top edge of the green sheet, overlapping it by about 3 inches. Working through both layers, attach two more grommets in each side of the flap, spacing the grommets about 4¾ to 5 inches apart on center. Continue attaching grommets through both sheets down the sides and across the bottom.

3 To make the flap closure, attach six pairs of grommets across the top edge of the plaid sheet (the bottom of the flap). Space the grommets in each pair about 1 inch apart and space the pairs about 10 to 12 inches apart. Attach six pairs of grommets in the top edge of the green sheet, aligning them with those in the flap edge (plaid sheet).

4 Measure the sides and bottom of the duvet cover. Cut two lengths of chenille yarn to that measurement. Starting at one top corner (with the flap folded down), thread the double strand of yarn through the grommets. Work down the side, across the bottom, and up the other side. At each top corner, thread the yarn ends through a wooden bead and knot the yarn ends.

5 Insert the comforter or duvet. Tie the flap closed by threading a 10-inch length of yarn through the pairs of grommets and making a bow (see the photo *top left*). Trim the yarn ends.

stitched version

1 To make the stitched version, trim 20 inches from the bottom of the green sheet and about 2½ inches from each side of both sheets (otherwise the cover will be too big for the duvet). From the 20-inch green strip, cut a 4¾-inch-wide strip. Press under ½ inch along both long edges; topstitch the strip to the right side of the plaid sheet's top edge to make a decorative border for the flap (see the photo *above right*).

2 Place the sheets (with the green sheet on top) with right sides facing and the bottom and side edges aligned. Fold the flap down over the top edge of the green sheet, overlapping it by 3 inches. Machine-stitch along the sides and bottom edges, using a ½-inch seam allowance. Turn the cover right side out. Attach heavy-duty snaps to the underside of the flap and also to the corresponding top edge of the green sheet. To decorate the flap border, stitch star-shaped novelty buttons over the snaps.

106

Privacy, Please

Turn the den or office into a private retreat for company with an easy-to-install curtain.

When you need the study, family room, or office to do double duty as guest quarters, you can still provide a feeling of privacy for visitors by closing off the sleeping area with folding screens or temporary curtains. A tension rod or shower-curtain rod can be inserted in a cased opening like the one shown here without damaging the woodwork. Slip a simple sleeved curtain over the rod, or cover it with a scrunched tube of fabric and tie fabric panels to the rod with ribbon.

Cheerful Touches

Give a holiday lift to your guest bath or a powder room, too. Bring out red and green hand towels and accent them with a perky gold bow. Fill a bowl with fragrant Christmas potpourri, and place a few pinecones on a bed of fresh greenery on the counter.

Midnight Snacks

Send your guests to bed with a tray of treats, or just keep these snacks handy for munching.

Lemon Bread

Place a few slices on a Christmas plate for the perfect accompaniment to a steaming hot drink.

½ cup butter
1 cup sugar
2 eggs
1⅔ cups all-purpose flour
¾ cup buttermilk
1½ teaspoons finely shredded
    lemon peel
½ teaspoon baking soda
¼ teaspoon salt
⅓ cup chopped almonds,
    walnuts, or pecans, toasted
    Lemon Glaze

Grease bottom and ½ inch up sides of two 7½×3½×2-inch loaf pans or one 8×4×2-inch loaf pan. Set aside.
Beat butter in a large mixing bowl with an electric mixer on medium speed about 30 seconds or until softened. Add the sugar and beat about 5 minutes or until light and fluffy. Add eggs, one at a time, beating until combined. Add flour, buttermilk, lemon peel, baking soda, and salt. Beat just until combined. Stir in nuts. Pour batter into prepared pan(s) and spread evenly.
Bake in a 350° oven about 40 minutes for 7½×3½×2-inch loaves and about 45 minutes for 8×4×2-inch loaf or until a wooden toothpick inserted near center(s) comes out clean. (If necessary, cover loosely with foil for the last 10 to 15 minutes of baking to prevent overbrowning.) Cool in pan(s) on wire rack for 10 minutes. Remove

from pan(s). Place on wire rack set over waxed paper.
Spoon Lemon Glaze over top(s). Cool completely on wire rack. Wrap and store overnight before slicing. Makes 2 small loaves or 1 large loaf (16 servings).
LEMON GLAZE: Stir together 3 tablespoons lemon juice and 1 tablespoon sugar in a small mixing bowl until sugar is dissolved.

Nutrition facts per serving: 174 cal., 8 g total fat (4 g sat. fat), 42 mg chol., 151 mg sodium, 24 g carbo., 1 g fiber, 3 g pro. Daily values: 6% vit. A, 2% vit. C, 2% calcium, 5% iron

Mexican Coffee

Use your coffeemaker to brew this lightly spiced, end-of-the-day beverage.

½ cup ground coffee
1 teaspoon ground cinnamon
⅛ teaspoon ground cloves
    Peel from 2 oranges
6 cups cold water
2 tablespoons brown sugar
    Orange peel twists (optional)

Line the coffee basket of an electric drip coffeemaker with a filter. Place coffee, cinnamon, cloves, and orange peel from the 2 oranges in the filter-lined basket. Pour cold water into water compartment; let water drip through basket into coffeepot. Stir sugar into coffee. Garnish with orange peel twists, if desired. Makes 8 servings.

Nutrition facts per serving: 16 cal., 0 g total fat (0 g sat. fat), 0 mg chol., 5 mg sodium, 4 g carbo., 0 g fiber, 0 g pro. Daily values: 0% vit. A, 3% vit. C, 1% calcium, 1% iron

Pumpkin Cream Cheese

Serve a small container of the cheese spread with a basket of split and toasted bagels for your guests to help themselves. Remember to include a spreader and napkins.

2 8-ounce packages cream
    cheese, softened
1 cup canned pumpkin
⅓ cup sugar
1½ teaspoons pumpkin pie spice
1 teaspoon vanilla

Beat cream cheese, pumpkin, sugar, pumpkin pie spice, and vanilla in a large mixing bowl with an electric mixer till smooth. Store tightly covered in the refrigerator. Serve as a spread for bagels. Makes about 3 cups.

Nutrition facts per tablespoon spread: 41 cal., 3 g total fat (2 g sat. fat), 10 mg chol., 29 mg sodium, 2 g carbo., 0 g fiber, 1 g pro. Daily values: 15% vit. A, 0% vit. C, 0% calcium, 1% iron

Spiced Pecans and Cherries

For a zippy snack to offer guests, try this fruit-and-nut combination.

2 tablespoons Worcestershire
    sauce
2 tablespoons butter, melted
½ teaspoon ground red pepper
½ teaspoon garlic powder
½ teaspoon ground cumin
½ teaspoon seasoned salt
¼ teaspoon dried oregano,
    crushed

Mexican Coffee

Lemon Bread

*Honey-Mustard
Pretzel Snacks*

3 cups pecan halves
1½ cups dried tart cherries

Stir together Worcestershire sauce, butter, red pepper, garlic powder, cumin, seasoned salt, and oregano. Add pecan halves, tossing to coat. Spread mixture in a 13×9×2-inch baking pan.
Bake in a 350° oven for 15 minutes; stir every 5 minutes. Stir in dried cherries. Bake 5 minutes more or until pecans are toasted. Spread on paper towels to cool. Store in an airtight container. Makes 4 cups.

Nutrition facts per ¼-cup serving: 188 cal., 15 g total fat (2 g sat. fat), 4 mg chol., 73 mg sodium, 13 g carbo., 2 g fiber, 2 g pro. Daily values: 8% vit. A, 6% vit. C, 0% calcium, 4% iron

Honey-Mustard
Pretzel Snacks

*Set out a container of this tasty snack
along with some chilled bottled water or
soft drinks for a late-night treat.*

¼ cup butter
¼ cup honey mustard
1 teaspoon Worcestershire sauce
¼ teaspoon garlic powder
    Several dashes bottled
        hot pepper sauce
10 cups small pretzels

Line a 15×10×1-inch baking pan with foil; set aside.

Melt butter in a small saucepan. Remove saucepan from heat and stir in honey mustard, Worcestershire sauce, garlic powder, and hot pepper sauce. Place pretzels in the prepared baking pan. Pour mustard mixture over pretzels; toss gently to coat.
Bake in a 300° oven for 25 minutes, stirring every 10 minutes. Spread on foil; cool. Store in an airtight container. Makes 10 cups.

Nutrition facts per ½-cup serving: 114 cal., 3 g total fat (2 g sat. fat), 6 mg chol., 407 mg sodium, 18 g carbo., 0 g fiber, 2 g pro. Daily values: 2% vit. A, 0% vit. C, 0% calcium, 2% iron

Yule Log

heavenly seven

We may count calories the rest of the year, but the holidays call for dazzling desserts.

☙ These recipes will supply a suitably spectacular ending to your holiday meal.

Yule Log
✳

1 cup all-purpose flour
¼ teaspoon salt
5 egg yolks
2 tablespoons sherry or milk
1 cup sugar
5 egg whites
¼ teaspoon cream of tartar
    Powdered sugar
    Coffee Cream Filling
    Rich Chocolate Frosting

Grease and lightly flour (or line with waxed paper and lightly grease) a 15×10×1-inch jelly-roll pan; set aside. Stir together flour and salt in a small bowl. Beat egg yolks and sherry in a medium mixing bowl with an electric mixer on high speed about 5 minutes or until thick and lemon-colored. Gradually add ½ cup of the sugar, beating until sugar is almost dissolved.
Wash beaters. Beat egg whites and cream of tartar in a large mixing bowl on medium to high speed until soft peaks form (tips curl). Gradually add remaining sugar, 2 tablespoons at a time, beating on medium to high speed until stiff peaks form (tips stand straight). Fold 1 cup of the egg-white mixture into egg-yolk mixture. Fold egg-yolk mixture into remaining egg-white mixture. Fold in flour mixture; spread in the prepared pan.
Bake in a 375° oven for 12 to 15 minutes or until top springs back. Immediately loosen cake from pan. Invert cake onto a towel sprinkled with powdered sugar. (Remove waxed paper if used.) Roll up warm cake and towel, jelly-roll style, starting from a short side. Cool on a wire rack.
Gently unroll cake. Spread filling on cake to within 1 inch of edges. Roll up cake without towel, jelly-roll style, starting from one of the short sides. Cut a 1½-inch slice from one end of cake. Frost cake with frosting. Place the slice on side of log to form a branch (see Photo 1); frost branch. Using tines of a fork, score cake lengthwise to resemble tree bark. Garnish with Chocolate-Covered Pinecones (see Photo 2), if desired. Makes 10 servings.

COFFEE CREAM FILLING: Beat 1 cup whipping cream, ¼ cup sifted powdered sugar, and 1½ teaspoons instant coffee crystals to soft peaks.
RICH CHOCOLATE FROSTING: Heat and stir 3 ounces unsweetened chocolate and 3 tablespoons butter in a saucepan until chocolate melts. Remove from heat. Stir in 1½ cups sifted powdered sugar, ¼ cup milk, and 1 teaspoon vanilla. Add 1½ cups additional powdered sugar and enough milk to make of spreading consistency (1 to 2 tablespoons).

Nutrition facts per serving: 449 cal., 20 g total fat (10 g sat. fat), 149 mg chol., 138 mg sodium, 66 g carbo., 1 g fiber, 6 g pro. Daily values: 31% vit. A, 0% vit. C, 3% calcium, 10% iron

111

here's how...

1. To add branch, cut off a 1½-inch slice from end of cake before frosting. Frost cake, put branch slice in place, and frost.
2. For Chocolate-Covered Pinecones: Shape a cone of almond paste about 1½ inches tall and 1 inch in diameter. Starting from wide end, insert halved or sliced almonds into cone. Melt together equal amounts of unsweetened and semisweet baking chocolate (not chocolate pieces) with a little shortening. Insert wooden picks into base of each cone. Hold over pan; spoon melted chocolate over to cover. Transfer to rack over waxed paper; let stand until firm.

White Cheesecake with
Raspberry Sauce

To prepare raspberry sauce, after
processing the thawed raspberries with a
food processor or blender, pour the
puree into a fine mesh sieve. Press
through the sieve into a small bowl,
using the back of a wooden spoon.
Discard the seeds from the sieve.

White Cheesecake
With Raspberry Sauce

1½ cups finely crushed
    chocolate sandwich cookies
3 tablespoons butter, melted
3 8-ounce packages cream
    cheese, softened
½ cup sugar
2 tablespoons all-purpose flour
1 teaspoon vanilla
2 egg whites
1 cup whipping cream
1 12-ounce package frozen lightly
    sweetened red raspberries,
    thawed
½ cup sugar
1 teaspoon lemon juice
Fresh raspberries (optional)
Mint leaves (optional)

For crust, combine crushed cookies
and butter. Press into bottom of an
8-inch springform pan. Combine cream
cheese, ½ cup sugar, the flour, and
vanilla in a large mixing bowl. Beat with
an electric mixer on medium speed
until fluffy. Add egg whites, one at a
time, beating on low speed just until
combined. Stir in whipping cream. Pour
into crust-lined pan. Place pan in a
shallow baking pan in oven.
Bake in a 375° oven for 40 to
45 minutes or until center appears
nearly set when gently shaken. Cool
15 minutes. Loosen crust from sides of

pan. Cool 30 minutes more; remove
sides of pan. Cool completely. Chill at
least 4 hours.
For sauce, place raspberries in food
processor bowl or blender container;
cover and process or blend just until
smooth. Press through a fine mesh
sieve (see photo, *above*). Discard seeds.
Combine puree, the ½ cup sugar, and
the lemon juice in a small saucepan.
Heat just until sugar dissolves; cool.
Cover and chill. Serve cheesecake with
sauce. If desired, garnish with a few
fresh raspberries and mint leaves.
Makes 12 servings.

Nutrition facts per serving: 442 cal., 33 g total fat
(20 g sat. fat), 98 mg chol., 295 mg sodium,
32 g carbo., 1 g fiber, 6 g pro. Daily values:
36% vit. A, 12% vit. C, 5% calcium, 7% iron

Tiramisu Cake

✳

This cake-style version of the Italian classic, Tiramisu, uses an angel cake mix or purchased cake instead of ladyfingers.

- 1 15-ounce package angel cake mix
- 1 8-ounce carton mascarpone cheese or one 8-ounce package cream cheese, softened
- ½ cup sifted powdered sugar
- 3 tablespoons coffee liqueur
- 2 cups whipping cream
- ¼ cup sifted powdered sugar
- 2 tablespoons coffee liqueur
- ¾ cup strong black coffee
- ¼ cup coffee liqueur
   Unsweetened cocoa powder, chocolate curls and/or chocolate designs, whipped cream, raspberries (optional)

Prepare the angel cake in a tube pan according to package directions. For filling, combine mascarpone cheese, the ½ cup powdered sugar, and the 3 tablespoons liqueur in a mixing bowl. Beat with an electric mixer until smooth. Set aside.

Combine whipping cream, the ¼ cup powdered sugar, and 2 tablespoons liqueur in a mixing bowl; beat until stiff peaks form. Fold ½ cup whipped cream mixture into mascarpone mixture. Set aside.

To assemble, cut cake horizontally into three even layers (see photo, *right*). Place first cake layer on a large serving plate. With a long-tine fork or skewers, poke holes in tops of each layer.

Combine coffee and the ¼ cup liqueur; drizzle over each cake layer. Spread half of the mascarpone filling on top of the first cake layer. Top with second cake layer, then spread with remaining mascarpone filling. Finally top with the remaining cake layer. Frost entire cake with remaining whipped cream mixture. If desired, cover and chill for up to 2 hours.

To serve, sprinkle slices lightly with unsweetened cocoa powder, if desired. Garnish with chocolate curls and/or chocolate designs, whipped cream, and raspberries, if desired. Cover any leftover cake and store in the refrigerator. Makes 16 servings.

Nutrition facts per serving: 354 cal., 19 g total fat (11 g sat. fat), 59 mg chol., 170 mg sodium, 40 g carbo., 0 g fiber, 8 g pro. Daily Values: 13% vit. A, 0% vit. C, 5% calcium, 3% iron

Tiramisu Cake

here's how...

To split the cake layers evenly, insert toothpicks to use as a guide, measuring an equal distance from the bottom or top of the cake. Use a long serrated blade knife to cut through the cake.

PASTRY FOR DOUBLE-CRUST PIE: Stir together 2 cups all-purpose flour and ½ teaspoon salt in a large mixing bowl. Using a pastry blender, cut in ⅔ cup shortening until pieces are the size of small peas. Sprinkle 1 tablespoon cold water over part of the mixture; gently toss. Push to side of bowl. Repeat with 5 to 7 additional tablespoons water, 1 tablespoon at a time, until all is moistened. Divide dough in half. Form each half into a ball.

Nutrition facts per serving: 464 cal., 18 g total fat (4 g sat. fat), 0 mg chol., 143 mg sodium, 75 g carbo., 2 g fiber, 4 g pro. Daily Values: 8% vit. A, 7% vit. C, 1% calcium, 19% iron

here's how...

To make an easy lattice top, place strips atop filling, beginning at opposite outside edges. Add crosswise strips beginning at outside edges.

114

Cranberry-Cherry Pie

2 16-ounce cans pitted tart red cherries (water pack)
1 cup cranberries
1½ cups sugar
¼ cup cornstarch
¼ teaspoon ground nutmeg
Dash ground cloves
Pastry for Double-Crust Pie
Sugared Cranberries (optional)
(see *page 102*)

Drain cherries, reserving ⅓ cup liquid. Combine reserved liquid and cranberries in a medium saucepan. Bring to boiling; reduce heat. Simmer, uncovered, for 3 minutes or until cranberries pop. Stir together ¾ cup of the sugar, the cornstarch, nutmeg, and cloves in a small bowl. Add to cranberries. Cook and stir until thickened and bubbly. Remove from

heat. Stir in remaining ¾ cup sugar and the cherries; set aside.

Prepare pastry. Slightly flatten one ball of dough on a lightly floured surface. Roll from center to edge, forming a 12-inch circle. Ease pastry into 9-inch pie plate. Trim pastry ½ inch beyond edge. Fold under extra pastry. Crimp edge. Do not prick.

Transfer cranberry-cherry mixture to pastry-lined pie plate. Roll out remaining dough. Using a fluted pastry wheel, if desired, cut eight 1¼-inch-wide strips. Make lattice atop pie, leaving an opening in center (see Photo 1). Cover edges of pastry with foil. Place pie in a shallow baking pan.

Bake in a 375° oven for 25 minutes. Remove foil. Bake 20 to 25 minutes more or until top is golden. Cool on a wire rack. If desired, garnish with Sugared Cranberries and baked leaves (see Photo 2). Makes 8 servings.

For leaf trim, cut leaf shapes from pastry scraps. Place cutouts on rolled up foil on baking sheet and sprinkle leaves with sugar. Bake in a 375° oven for 10 to 12 minutes. Arrange on baked pie.

Chocolate-Chip Nut Tart

To shortcut preparations, substitute a refrigerated unbaked piecrust for the pastry. Roll out and ease into pan.

Pastry for Single-Crust Tart
3 eggs
1 cup light-colored corn syrup
½ cup packed brown sugar
⅓ cup butter, melted and cooled
1 teaspoon vanilla
1 cup coarsely chopped salted mixed nuts
½ cup miniature semisweet chocolate pieces
⅓ cup miniature semisweet chocolate pieces
1 tablespoon shortening

Prepare pastry. Roll pastry from center to edge on lightly floured surface, forming a 12-inch circle. Ease pastry into an 11-inch tart pan with removable bottom. Trim pastry to rim of pan. Do not prick.

For filling, beat eggs slightly with a whisk or fork in large mixing bowl. Stir in corn syrup. Stir in brown sugar, butter, and vanilla until sugar dissolves. Stir in nuts and the ½ cup chocolate pieces. Place pastry-lined tart pan on baking sheet on oven rack. Carefully pour filling into pan.

Bake in a 350° oven for 40 minutes or until a knife inserted near the center comes out clean. Cool on wire rack.

To serve, remove sides of pan; cut tart into wedges. Place the ⅓ cup chocolate pieces and the shortening in a small heavy saucepan over very low heat; stir constantly until chocolate begins to melt. Remove from heat; stir until smooth. Cool to room temperature. Drizzle across each wedge (see Photos 1 and 2). Serve with scoop of vanilla ice cream, if desired. Makes 12 servings.

PASTRY FOR SINGLE-CRUST TART: Stir together 1¼ cups all-purpose flour and ¼ teaspoon salt in a medium bowl. Using a pastry blender, cut in ⅓ cup shortening until pieces are the size of small peas. Sprinkle 1 tablespoon cold water over part of the mixture; gently toss. Push to side of bowl. Repeat with 3 to 4 additional tablespoons water, 1 tablespoon at a time, until all is moistened. Form the dough into a ball.

Nutrition facts per serving: 398 cal., 22 g total fat (6 g sat. fat), 67 mg chol., 135 mg sodium, 48 g carbo., 1 g fiber, 5 g pro. Daily values: 7% vit. A, 0% vit. C, 3% calcium, 18% iron

Chocolate-Chip Nut Tart

here's how...

1 For easy decorating, transfer melted and cooled chocolate to a small self-sealing plastic bag that is set into a glass or bowl. Snip a small hole in the corner of the chocolate-filled bag.

2 Drizzle chocolate over individual servings of the dessert in a zigzag line, letting some of the chocolate flow onto the dessert plate.

115

Remove from heat. Combine about ¼ cup of the hot cream, 2 egg yolks, and ½ cup granulated sugar in a bowl. Beat with an electric mixer on high speed for 2 to 3 minutes or until thick and lemon-colored. Gradually stir about half of the remaining cream into yolk mixture. Return all of the yolk mixture to saucepan. Cook and stir over medium heat just until mixture returns to boiling. Remove from heat. Stir in 1 teaspoon vanilla and, if desired, 1 tablespoon amaretto.

Nutrition facts per serving: 345 cal., 19 g total fat (10 g sat. fat), 125 mg chol., 21 mg sodium, 43 g carbo., 3 g fiber, 3 g pro. Daily values: 28% vit. A, 14% vit. C, 5% calcium, 5% iron

Poached Pears with Almonds

here's how...

Poached Pears with Almonds

✳

Toast the almonds ahead of time, but allow for last-minute preparation to make the elegant presentation of this fruit dessert.

⅓ cup packed brown sugar
¼ cup orange juice
½ teaspoon ground nutmeg
1 tablespoon amaretto or
   ¼ teaspoon almond extract
3 ripe large pears
   Crème Anglaise
3 tablespoons sliced almonds,
   toasted
   Ground nutmeg

Stir together sugar, orange juice, and the ½ teaspoon nutmeg in a large skillet. Cook and stir over low heat until sugar is melted. Stir in amaretto; set caramel-orange mixture aside.

Cut pears in half lengthwise, leaving stems intact on a half of each pear.

Remove core; peel pear halves. Place pear halves on a cutting board and make about 7 lengthwise cuts in each half (see photo, *right*). Transfer pears, flat sides down, to skillet with caramel-orange mixture. Spoon mixture over pears. Bring to boiling; reduce heat. Cover and simmer for 6 to 8 minutes or until pears are tender, occasionally spooning mixture over pears. Prepare the Crème Anglaise.

Carefully remove pears from skillet; transfer to individual dishes. Gently boil caramel-orange liquid for 3 to 4 minutes or until reduced to half (about 3 tablespoons).

To serve, pour warm Crème Anglaise around pears in dishes. Drizzle the caramel-orange mixture on top of the Crème Anglaise. Sprinkle with almonds and additional ground nutmeg. Makes 6 servings.

CRÈME ANGLAISE: Bring 1 cup whipping cream just to boiling in a heavy saucepan, stirring frequently.

To slice pears, place the peeled, cored pear half, flat side down, on a cutting board. Starting about ½ inch from stem end and cutting to bottom of pear, make 7 lengthwise cuts in each half as shown.

Raspberry Truffle Cake

12 ounces semisweet chocolate,
      cut up
½   cup whipping cream
¼   cup butter
½   cup sugar
 1   tablespoon all-purpose flour
 4   egg yolks
 4   egg whites
¾   cup seedless raspberry jam
      Sweetened Whipped Cream
      Fresh raspberries (optional)
      Chocolate curls (optional)
      (see page 103)

Grease an 8-inch springform pan. Line bottom of the pan with parchment paper and grease the paper. Set aside.

Combine chocolate, whipping cream, and butter in a large heavy saucepan. Cook and stir over low heat until chocolate melts. Remove from heat. Stir in sugar and flour. With a wooden spoon, beat in egg yolks, one at a time, just until combined; set aside.

Beat egg whites in a large mixing bowl with an electric mixer on high speed until stiff peaks form. Gently fold about 1 cup of the beaten egg whites into the chocolate mixture (see photo, *right*). Fold chocolate mixture into remaining beaten egg whites. Pour mixture into prepared pan.

Bake in a 325° oven for 30 to 35 minutes or until puffed and set about 2 inches around edges. Cool the cake in the pan on a wire rack for 30 minutes. Remove sides of pan and cool for 4 hours. Chill 4 to 24 hours.

Remove cake from parchment and place on serving platter just before serving. Heat jam just until melted. Top cake with Sweetened Whipped Cream, raspberries, and chocolate curls. To serve, cut into wedges, wiping knife between slices to prevent dessert from sticking to the knife. Drizzle each wedge with 1 tablespoon melted jam. Makes 12 servings.

SWEETENED WHIPPED CREAM: Chill mixing bowl and beaters of electric mixer in refrigerator. Combine 1 cup whipping cream, 2 tablespoons powdered sugar, and ½ teaspoon vanilla in the chilled bowl. Beat with chilled beaters on medium speed until soft peaks form. Makes 2 cups.

Nutrition facts per serving: 390 cal., 26 g total fat (15 g sat. fat), 122 mg chol., 74 mg sodium, 42 g carbo., 2 g fiber, 5 g pro. Daily values: 27% vit. A, 0% vit. C, 3% calcium, 9% iron

Raspberry Truffle Cake

here's how...

A folding hint: To keep the mixture as light as possible, fold some of the stiffly beaten egg whites into the chocolate mixture to lighten the texture. Then fold the chocolate mixture into the remaining beaten egg whites.

coffee
break

*Heartwarming
Cinnamon-Orange
Coffee Cake*

Keep these make-ahead coffee cakes on hand. When it's time for a well-deserved break with a friend, serve one with a flavored coffee or tea (see *page 121*).

Heartwarming Cinnamon-Orange Coffee Cake

4 to 4½ cups all-purpose flour
2 packages active dry yeast
½ cup milk
⅓ cup sugar
⅓ cup butter
1 teaspoon salt
2 eggs
½ cup orange juice
2 tablespoons finely shredded
    orange peel
3 tablespoons butter, melted
½ cup sugar
½ cup coconut (optional)
2 teaspoons ground cinnamon
    Orange Glaze

Stir together 2 cups of the flour and yeast in a large mixing bowl; set aside. Heat and stir milk, the ⅓ cup sugar, ⅓ cup butter, and salt in a medium saucepan until warm (120° to 130°) and butter almost melts. Add to flour mixture. Add eggs and orange juice. Beat with an electric mixer on low to medium speed for 30 seconds, scraping sides of the bowl. Beat on high speed for 3 minutes. Using a wooden spoon, stir in orange peel and as much of the remaining flour as you can.
Turn dough out onto a lightly floured surface. Knead in enough of the remaining flour to make a moderately soft dough that is smooth and elastic (3 to 5 minutes). Shape dough into a ball. Place dough in a lightly greased

bowl, turning once to grease surface. Cover and let rise in a warm place until double in size (about 1½ hours).
Punch dough down. Turn dough out onto a lightly floured surface. Divide dough in half. Cover and let rest 10 minutes.
Roll each half of dough into a 15×10-inch rectangle. Brush each rectangle with half of the melted butter.
Combine the ½ cup sugar, the coconut (if using), and cinnamon. Sprinkle half of the sugar mixture over each dough rectangle.
Roll up each rectangle, jelly-roll style, starting from one of the long sides. Pinch seams to seal. Place seam side up on greased baking sheets. Fold half of each roll over the top of its other half, sealing ends. Starting 1½ inches from the sealed end, cut all the way though the dough to the folded end (see Photo 1). Turn cut sides out so they

face up, forming a heart shape (see Photo 2). Cover; let rise in a warm place until nearly double (30 minutes).
Bake in a 375° oven about 20 minutes or until lightly browned. Remove from baking sheets; place on wire racks to cool slightly. Drizzle with Orange Glaze, unless freezing. Serve warm or cool. (To make ahead, freeze the unfrosted baked coffee cakes tightly wrapped. To serve, wrap frozen coffee cakes in foil and heat in a 300° oven about 25 minutes or until warm. Drizzle with Orange Glaze.) Makes 24 servings.
ORANGE GLAZE: Stir together 1 cup sifted powdered sugar and 1 teaspoon finely shredded orange peel in a small mixing bowl. Stir in enough orange juice (1 to 2 tablespoons) to make a frosting of drizzling consistency.

Nutrition facts per serving: 162 cal., 5 g total fat (3 g sat. fat), 29 mg chol., 138 mg sodium, 27 g carbo., 1 g fiber, 3 g pro. Daily values: 4% vit. A, 6% vit. C, 1% calcium, 7% iron

here's how...

1

Work on the greased baking sheet. Start from the sealed end and slice through the dough layers using a sharp knife. Steady the roll as you cut with your other hand.

2

Gently open the cut. Carefully lay each side flat on the baking sheet with the cut sides facing up and touching each other. The dough will form a heart shape on the baking sheet.

Café Mocha

Gingerbread Mini-Loaves with Nutmeg Glaze

⅓ cup butter
⅓ cup packed brown sugar
1 egg
½ cup boiling water
⅓ cup mild-flavored molasses
1⅔ cups all-purpose flour
2 teaspoons baking powder
1¼ teaspoons ground ginger
1 teaspoon ground cinnamon
¼ teaspoon baking soda
⅛ teaspoon salt
⅛ teaspoon ground cloves
Nutmeg Glaze
2 tablespoons finely
chopped walnuts

Grease bottom and ½ inch up the sides of four 4½×2½×1½-inch or three 5¾×3×2-inch loaf pans. Set pans aside.
Beat butter in a medium mixing bowl with an electric mixer on medium speed about 30 seconds or until softened. Add brown sugar and beat until light and fluffy. Add egg and beat until combined.
Combine boiling water and molasses in a small bowl; add to brown sugar mixture, beating at low speed until combined. Combine flour, baking powder, ginger, cinnamon, baking soda, salt, and cloves in a medium mixing bowl. Add to molasses mixture, beating just until combined. Spread batter in prepared pans.
Bake in a 350° oven about 30 minutes or until a wooden toothpick inserted near centers comes out clean. Cool in pans on wire racks for 10 minutes. Remove from pans. Cool completely on wire racks. Wrap and

Overnight Stollen Coffee Cake

⅔ cup butter
1 cup granulated sugar
2 eggs
1 8-ounce carton dairy sour
cream
1 teaspoon vanilla
2 cups all-purpose flour
1 teaspoon baking powder
½ teaspoon baking soda
½ teaspoon salt
½ cup raisins
½ cup red candied cherries,
chopped
½ cup green candied cherries,
chopped
½ cup packed brown sugar
½ teaspoon ground cinnamon
½ cup chopped pecans

Beat butter and granulated sugar in a medium mixing bowl with an electric mixer on medium-high speed until light and fluffy. Add eggs, sour cream, and vanilla; beat until well combined. Stir together flour, baking powder, baking soda, and salt. Add to sugar mixture; beat until combined. Stir in raisins and ⅓ cup each of the red and green cherries (reserve remaining cherries for topping). Pour batter into a greased 13×9×2-inch baking pan.
Stir together brown sugar, cinnamon, pecans, and reserved cherries; sprinkle evenly over batter. Cover and refrigerate overnight.
Bake in a 350° oven, uncovered, for 35 to 40 minutes. Serve warm or cooled. Makes 12 to 16 servings.

Nutrition facts per serving: 399 cal., 18 g total fat (9 g sat. fat), 71 mg chol., 299 mg sodium, 57 g carbo., 1 g fiber, 4 g pro. Daily values: 15% vit. A, 0% vit. C, 6% calcium, 10% iron

store overnight. Before serving, drizzle with Nutmeg Glaze. Sprinkle with nuts. Makes 3 or 4 loaves (18 servings).

NUTMEG GLAZE: Stir together ⅔ cup sifted powdered sugar, 2 teaspoons apple cider or apple juice, and ¼ teaspoon ground nutmeg in a small mixing bowl. Stir in a little additional apple cider or apple juice, if necessary, to make of drizzling consistency.

Nutrition facts per serving: 123 cal., 4 g total fat (1 g sat. fat), 16 mg chol., 110 mg sodium, 20 g carbo., 0 g fiber, 2 g pro. Daily values: 3% vit. A, 0% vit. C, 4% calcium, 6% iron

Café Mocha

The sugar squiggles melt gradually and sweeten your coffee as they dissolve.

1⅓ cups milk
¼ cup chocolate-flavored syrup
1⅓ cups hot espresso or very
    strong coffee (brewed or
    instant)
    Whipped cream (optional)
4 Spun-Sugar Squiggles (optional)

Heat milk in a heavy saucepan until it just comes to boiling. Remove from heat and beat with a rotary beater until the milk is frothy.

Place 1 tablespoon of the chocolate-flavored syrup in each of 4 cups. Add hot espresso, then hot milk to each cup. Stir to mix. Dollop each serving with whipped cream and top with a Spun-Sugar Squiggle, if desired. Serves 4.

SPUN-SUGAR SQUIGGLES: Line a baking sheet with foil. Heat 2 tablespoons sugar in a small skillet over medium-high heat (do not stir) until sugar begins to melt, shaking skillet occasionally to heat evenly. Reduce heat to low; continue cooking until sugar is melted and turns golden brown, stirring occasionally with a

wooden spoon. Quickly drizzle the caramelized sugar onto foil, making lacy patterns. When cool, carefully peel sugar from foil and break into 1½-inch pieces. Float squiggles atop whipped-cream-topped coffee. Makes enough to garnish 6 to 8 cups of coffee.

Nutrition facts per serving: 83 cal., 2 g total fat (1 g sat. fat), 6 mg chol., 52 mg sodium, 15 g carbo., 0 g fiber, 3 g pro. Daily values: 4% vit. A, 1% vit. C, 8% calcium, 2% iron

Orange-Anise Coffee

½ cup ground coffee
2 teaspoons finely shredded
    orange peel
2 teaspoons brown sugar
1 teaspoon aniseed
8 cups cold water
    Half-and-half or light cream
    (optional)

Line the coffee basket of an electric drip coffeemaker with a filter. Place coffee, orange peel, brown sugar, and aniseed in the basket. Pour cold water into water compartment; let water drip through basket into coffeepot. Serve with half-and half or light cream, if desired. Makes 10 servings.

Nutrition facts per serving: 8 cal., 0 g total fat (0 g sat. fat), 0 mg chol., 4 mg sodium, 2 g carbo., 0 g fiber, 0 g pro. Daily values: 0% vit. A, 0% vit. C, 0% calcium, 1% iron

Hot Tea with Lemon

8 cups water
½ cup sugar
8 inches stick cinnamon, broken
1 12-ounce can frozen pineapple-
    orange juice concentrate
1 6-ounce can frozen
    lemonade concentrate
6 tea bags

Combine 2 cups of the water, the sugar, and cinnamon sticks in a large pot or Dutch oven. Bring to boiling, stirring until sugar is dissolved. Stir in remaining 6 cups water, frozen pineapple-orange juice concentrate, and frozen lemonade concentrate. Heat through. Remove saucepan from heat; remove cinnamon sticks. Add tea bags to saucepan. Cover and let steep for 5 minutes. Remove and discard tea bags. Serve tea at once. Makes about 12 (6-ounce) servings.

Nutrition facts per serving: 111 cal., 0 g total fat (0 g sat. fat), 0 mg chol., 6 mg sodium, 28 g carbo., 0 g fiber, 0 g pro. Daily values: 0% vit. A, 26% vit. C, 1% calcium, 1% iron

Cranberry Spiced Tea

6 inches stick cinnamon, broken
1 teaspoon whole cloves
1 teaspoon whole allspice
1 cup water
¼ cup sugar
4 cups apple cider or apple juice
3 cups strong brewed tea
1 12-ounce can frozen cranberry-
    orange juice cocktail
    concentrate

For spice bag, place broken stick cinnamon, cloves, and allspice on a double-thickness 6-inch square of 100% cotton cheesecloth. Bring corners together and tie with a clean kitchen string. Set spice bag aside.

Combine water and sugar in a saucepan. Bring to boiling, stirring until sugar is dissolved. Stir in spice bag, apple cider or apple juice, tea, and frozen concentrate. Heat through, but do not boil. Discard spice bag. Makes 12 (6-ounce) servings.

Nutrition facts per serving: 109 cal., 0 g total fat (0 g sat. fat), 0 mg chol., 6 mg sodium, 28 g carbo., 0 g fiber, 0 g pro. Daily values: 0% vit. A, 38% vit. C, 0% calcium, 2% iron

121

GIVING

It's true: Presentation *is* everything.

Even a simple gift seems special when you present it in a box or bag you've dressed up with rubber stamps, tin stars, or metallic confetti. You don't have to be a crafter to ensure that your good things come in interesting packages—just tap your own creativity and let the ideas on the following pages inspire you. The same goes for gifts: Whether it's a jar of homemade fudge sauce, a basket of potted plants, or a themed collection of purchased items, it's the creativity and thought that count, carrying a special message of affection. You don't think you're creative? That's okay. Just follow our step-by-step instructions or take a cue from our ideas for "Instant Gifts" on *pages 138–39.* When you put your heart into it, it's as much fun to give as it is to receive.

from the HEART

SHOPPING LIST
FOR MESH BOW:
6 feet of fiberglass
    screening (window
    screening), available at
    hardware stores
gold spray paint
floral wire or crafts wire

SHOPPING LIST
FOR TIN STAR:
6-inch square piece of
    28-gauge tin
tracing paper
6-inch square of
    lightweight cardboard
    for pattern
scrap of wood at least
    7 inches square
tin snips
roofing nails
16d (sixteen-penny) nail or
    small nail punch
cold chisels in $\frac{3}{16}$ and
    $\frac{3}{8}$-inch widths
rubber or wooden mallet
fine steel wool
nonglossy primer or
    paint for metal
lightweight floral wire

A beautifully wrapped gift is a treat to receive—and a treat to give. With just a little creativity, you can turn ordinary materials into extraordinary packaging.

wrap it up

For a homespun look, use brown wrapping paper and add a punched-tin star or a bow of fiberglass window screening. For a more celestial effect, use rubber stamps and embossing powder to transform plain paper bags into elegant containers. Adorn Hanukkah gifts with glittering Stars of David. If you've got a large or odd-shaped gift, try the creative cover-up on *page 127*.

tin star

here's how...

1 Enlarge the half-star pattern on *page 127* by 200 percent and trace it (including the dots and lines) onto the tracing paper. Flip the paper to trace the other half, making a complete star.

2 Tape the tracing paper to the cardboard and press over all marks with a pencil to transfer the shape. Cut out the cardboard star and punch through the dots and along the interior lines. Trace around the template on the tin with an awl or pencil, and mark the dots and lines for the design.

Cut out the star with tin snips. Use caution; the edges will be sharp. You may want to wear heavy gloves. Also clip off the tip of each point to lessen the chance of cutting yourself.

Fasten the star to the wood scrap by tacking roofing nails along the edges in several spots. To make the design, pierce

the star at each dot, using a 16d nail or a nail punch and hammer. Practice on a scrap of tin first. To cut the slots, pierce the tin at each line with the appropriate-size chisel.

5 If the star bends as you work on it, gently flatten it from the back with a mallet. Buff both sides with steel wool. Work carefully; the edges of the punched lines and holes are sharp.

6 Either leave the tin its natural color or paint it with a nonglossy primer or paint for metal. Thread wire through two holes, bringing both ends to the back, to attach the star to a package.

mesh bow

here's how...

1 Spray each side of the screening gold, letting the paint dry between coats. Cut the screening into strips 3 to 5 inches wide and about 6 feet long. The wider the strip, the bigger and showier the bow will be.

2 Wrap one strip around a package; cut off the excess. Loop and twist a strip to make a bow, securing the loops with wire. Trim the streamers as desired.

3 To make the center rosette, use a strip about 3 inches wide by 2 feet long. Gathering up one long edge with your fingers, roll the strip loosely, pinching together the gathered edge as you work. Let the top edge fan out slightly. When the rosette reaches the desired size, cut off the excess material and wrap the base of the rosette tightly with wire. Wire the rosette to the center of the bow and wire the bow to the package. If you wish, glue pine, dried leaves, and pinecones under the bow. To give the materials a verdigris look, mist them with patina-green and gold spray paints.

125

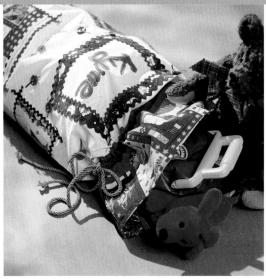

Hanukkah Surprises

Gifts sparkle with star-shaped confetti.

 Dress up packages with white wire-edge ribbon tied into fluffy bows, and attach Star-of-David confetti with dots of hot glue. (Check paper- and party-goods stores for the confetti.) Drop a handful of the stars into a clear cellophane bag with menorah candles and tie the bag closed with silver cording. To make the standing star, brush clear-drying glue on a blue plastic star and sprinkle it with silver glitter. Glue the star to a bow.

gift sack

(shown on *page 124*)

■ Spray the screening gold as for the mesh bow. Cut a strip wide enough for your gift to fit and twice as long. Fold the strip in half so the folded edge is the base of the bag.

■ Using yarn, floss, or ribbon and a large-eyed needle, blanket-stitch the edges of the screening together. Blanket-stitch around the opening. Tie the bag closed with yarn.

Santa's Sack

Turn a king-size pillowcase into a personalized bag from Santa.

here's how...

1 Wash and dry all fabrics, trims, and the pillowcase. To make the band for the top of the sack, use the holiday-print fabric and cut a strip 14 inches wide and twice the width of the pillowcase opening plus 1 inch. To make the best use of the fabric's design, position the band so it shows one or more rows of the design. With right sides facing, stitch the short ends of the strip together with a ½-inch seam. Trim the seam allowances. Iron fusible web to the wrong side of the fabric, following the manufacturer's instructions and piecing as necessary.

2 Fold the band in half lengthwise, wrong sides facing, and finger press. Fuse the band to the top of the pillowcase, enclosing the pillowcase's decorative edge. On some pillowcases, the decorative edge is slightly shaped so the top is wider than the case. You will need to make small pleats at the bottom of the band to fit it to the pillowcase.

3 To make the drawstring casing, center the narrow grosgrain ribbon on the wide grosgrain ribbon and stitch it in place close to the edges of the narrow ribbon. Pin the casing to the pillowcase, overlapping the raw edges of the band. Turn under and overlap the raw ends of the casing, leaving the ends of the narrow ribbon open to receive the cord. Stitch the casing in place.

4 Paint or write the child's name on the pillowcase with a fabric marker or fabric paint. An easy way to do this is to use a computer to print the name, then place the pattern under the pillowcase to use as a guide. Heat-set the paint or ink if necessary, following the manufacturer's instructions. Outline the letters with the fine-point permanent marker.

5 Cut a frame for the name from the companion fabric, making the inside dimensions of the frame 1 inch larger on all sides than the name and 1¼ inches wide on all sides. Use fusible web to attach the frame to the fabric. Cut rickrack to fit the inside and outside dimensions of the name frame, and glue the rickrack in place with fabric glue.

6 Iron fusible web to the remaining decorative fabric and cut the fabric into blocks. Fuse the blocks to the pillowcase, placing them randomly. Cut lengths of rickrack 2½ inches longer than each side of the blocks, and glue the rickrack to the blocks, letting the ends hang free.

7 Using narrow satin ribbon and the large-eyed needle, sew buttons to each corner of the name frame. Tie the ribbon ends over the center of each button and trim the ends to 1 inch. Sew the remaining buttons randomly to the pillowcase in the same way. Run the cord through the casing; knot the ends and dip them in fabric glue to keep them from fraying.

Canvas Cover-Up

Transform an ordinary canvas drop cloth into a whimsical wrap for large or unwieldy gifts.

The lucky recipient can use the cloth as a holiday table covering!

here's how...

1 Draw a star (or enlarge the one *at left* and use it as a guide) and trace it onto the sponge. Cut out the shape with the utility knife. To make the dot stamp, trace the top of the paint container on a scrap of sponge, and cut it out.

2 Spread the plastic drop cloth on your work surface, then lay the canvas drop cloth over it. Lightly mark the canvas to indicate where the zigzags will go. Pour a small amount of paint into a pie pan or disposable plate, and thin it with a few drops of water so the sponge can easily absorb it.

3 Begin stamping the stars in the center of the canvas and work out

toward the edges, placing the stars randomly. For each image, dip the star sponge into the paint, then press it onto the canvas.

4 Using the polyester brush, paint zigzag lines along the border. Stamp red dots along the edges of the canvas under every other zigzag.

5 After the paint has dried, use the green marker to draw swirls randomly among the stars. Also outline the red zigzags along the borders and write "Merry Christmas" as often as desired in the remaining spaces between the stars.

6 Drape or wrap the cloth over your gift and tie it with upholstery cord or wide ribbon.

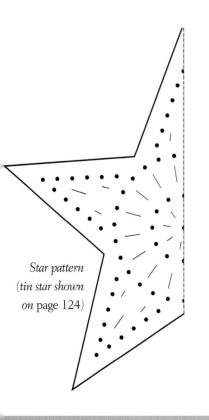

Star pattern (tin star shown on page 124)

Embossed Gift Bags

Rubber stamps and embossing powder transform
ordinary paper bags into elegant packaging.

129

Use the electric embossing tool to heat
the powder until it melts, forming an
embossed design. You can also hold the
stamped design over a toaster or the eye
of an electric stove to melt the powder,
but the tool is faster and more effective.
Repeat this procedure to decorate the
bag with as many images as you like.

here's how...

1 Ink the embossing pad with clear ink. Press the
rubber stamp onto the pad, then onto the paper
bag, being careful not to wiggle the stamp.

SHOPPING LIST

**From a crafts store or
rubber-stamp store:**
- rubber stamps
- clear embossing ink
  and embossing pad
- silver, gold, and blue
  metallic embossing
  powders
- electric embossing tool
- plain white paper sacks

design tips...

■ Stamp bags with
stars of different sizes
and in different colors.
To close the bags, use
a star-shaped hole
punch to make holes
for ribbon or a gilded
twig. Or, use sealing
wax and a seal to
secure the bag.
■ To decorate a
papier-mâché box,
paint it white and
stamp it with gold
metallic acrylic paint.

3 Shake off the excess powder; use a soft, dry
paintbrush to clean the background around the
design if necessary.

2 Working quickly, while the ink is wet,
sprinkle embossing powder in the
desired color over the stamped image.

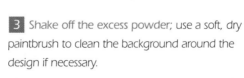

Convey your heartfelt feelings with a handmade gift. Or, if you're pressed for time, assemble an "instant gift" tailored to the recipient's tastes and interests; see *pages 138–39* for ideas.

tokens of
affection

see *pages 138–39* for ideas.

family traditions

M y husband and I were anticipating our baby's first Christmas when we realized opening gifts wouldn't be that much fun—our infant was too young to be excited about the toys, and we'd know everything our child was getting. We decided to divide the Christmas allowance between us, shop separately, and keep the baby's presents a secret from each other. We had so much fun surprising each other that we've decided to continue this method until the baby is older.

— *Sandi Hutchinson, Stillwell, Kansas*

131

SHOPPING LIST

From a crafts store:
decorative 16-ounce bottle with cork
assorted dried flowers
raffia

From a bed-and-bath shop, nature store, or gift shop:
16 ounces of almond oil (for Soothing Bath Oil)
16 ounces of soy oil, safflower oil, sunflower oil, olive oil, or wheat-germ oil (for Stimulating Bath Oil)
essential oils: lavender, rose, rosemary, juniper
vitamin E capsules
funnel, large coffee can, and saucepan
paraffin (available in grocery stores)

Aromatic Bath Oils

Choose lavender for a soothing bath oil or juniper for one that leaves you feeling invigorated. The dried flowers are just for looks—the fragrances come from the essential oils.

here's how...

1 Wash the bottle in hot, soapy water, rinse, and let it dry. Stuff dried flowers into the bottle for decoration.

2 Blend the oils in a separate container. For Soothing Bath Oil, mix the almond oil with 24 drops of lavender essential oil and 8 drops of rose essential oil. For the Stimulating Bath Oil, blend the carrier oil (soy oil or one of the suggested substitutes) with 24 drops of rosemary essential oil and 8 drops of juniper essential oil. For each mixture, break open 8 capsules of vitamin E and stir the contents into the oil mixture.

3 Using the funnel, pour the oil mixture into the bottle and cork it. To seal the cork with paraffin, place the wax in the coffee can and stand the can in a saucepan with several inches of water. Bring the water to simmering and let the paraffin melt. Dip the corked top into the melted paraffin several times to seal it and keep the closure airtight. Tie additional dried flowers to the neck of the bottle with raffia.

132

Basket of Flowers

Give a living gift of potted plants in a
moss-covered basket.

SHOPPING LIST
10-inch diameter clay pot
sheet moss
hot-glue gun and
    glue sticks
flexible branches about
    ¼ inch in diameter and
    3 feet long
pruning shears
spool wire (from a crafts
    store or floral supply
    shop)
live plants in 4-inch pots
fresh herbs

∾ It makes a wonderful fresh
arrangement, and the potted plants can
be replaced to change with the seasons.

Use the hot-glue gun to attach pads of sheet moss
to the sides and top edges of the pot.

Bend the rope over the pot, positioning
each end flush with the bottom of the
pot. Hold it in place by wrapping the pot
and sticks with spool wire.

133

To make the basket handle, cut long flexible
branches ¼ inch or less in diameter (willow and
birch are especially easy to work with). Weave the
branches together or align several and wrap them
with spool wire to make a rope 6 to 8 feet long.

Use spool wire to tie bunches of herbs into
bouquets, assembling three or more kinds of herbs
with contrasting textures in each bundle. Position
the potted plants in the moss-covered pot. Wrap the
stem ends of the herb bouquets in damp moss,
then tuck them in among the potted plants.

Wire additional
stems of herbs to
the basket handle,
and cover the wire
with ribbon.

Recipe Box

Fill this easy-to-make box with your favorite recipes for a wonderful keepsake gift.

❧ Be sure to include old family recipes—the collection will make a cherished gift for children or grandchildren setting up housekeeping.

here's how...

1 Following the diagram *below right*, draw a pattern on tracing paper. Cut out and trace onto the wrong side of the corrugated paper. Cut out the shape.

2 Lightly score the paper along the dashed lines. To score, lightly draw a crafts knife across the right side of the paper, using a ruler as a guide; you want to indent the paper to make a sharp fold, but don't cut all the way through. Fold the paper along the scored lines.

3 Glue the red card stock onto the bottom of the box. Glue one 6½-inch flap to the sides to create a pocket for the recipe cards.

4 Using the hole punch, make holes where indicated by Xs on the pattern. Place a cinnamon stick in the center of a 5-inch piece of raffia and wrap the raffia around the stick twice. Center the stick between the holes on the right side of one flap and slip the raffia ends through the holes to the inside. Knot the raffia ends and clip the excess. Repeat for the remaining flap. After you fill the box with recipe cards, close the flaps and wrap the 16-inch length of raffia figure-eight style around both cinnamon sticks.

SHOPPING LIST

From a crafts store:
tracing paper, ruler, and scissors
8x15-inch piece of corrugated paper
crafts knife and hole punch
4¼x6¼-inch rectangle of red card stock
thick white crafts glue
two 5-inch lengths of raffia
two 2-inch pieces of cinnamon sticks
16 inches of raffia

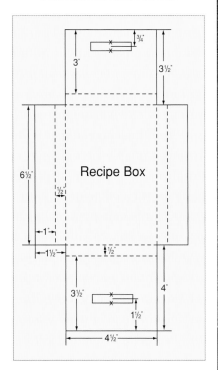

Recipe Box

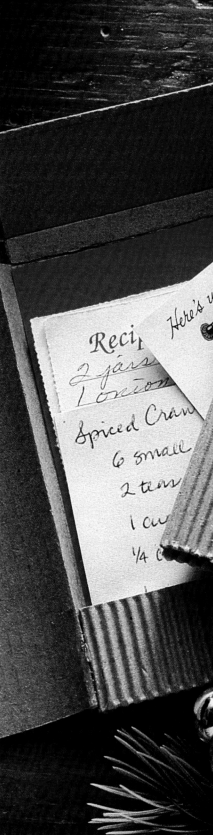

From an art-supply store:
one sheet of handmade
    paper 20×30 inches
eight 20×26-inch sheets
    of heavy art paper
spray adhesive
scraps of black and
    gold art papers

From a crafts store:
crafts knife and
    hole punch
2¾×9-inch scrap
    of leather
white glue

From a hardware store:
⅞-inch diameter
    O rings
16-inch length of brass
    rod or tubing,
    cut in half
two 9×12-inch envelopes
4 feet of ¼-inch-wide
    grosgrain ribbon
old family photo
crochet hook

136

family traditions

Every year on January 1, we spend the day putting the past year's photographs into an album. It's hard to keep up with this job during the year, but New Year's Day is usually a stay-at-home day for us, so it's fun to look over the year's events while organizing the photos and putting them in the album.

—— *Linda Gnesin*
Cherry Hill, New Jersey

Memory Album

Along with pages for photos, this album includes envelopes bound in to hold memorabilia—theater tickets, greeting cards, letters, pressed flowers, and other mementoes.

❧ For the bound-in envelopes, use purchased 9×12-inch envelopes, or make your own from art paper. Open up a purchased envelope and use it as a pattern. Glue hook-and-loop fastening-tape dots to the flap and envelope.

here's how...

1 To make the album pages, cut the heavy art paper into 12 sheets measuring 9×14 inches. On each page, score 1 inch in from one short edge. To score paper, draw the crafts knife lightly across the surface of the paper, using the ruler as a guide. Fold the paper to the front along the scored line. To deckle the opposite short edge, hold the ruler firmly on the paper about 2 inches from the edge and carefully tear the paper along the ruler.

2 To make the covers, cut two 9×24½-inch rectangles from the hand-made paper. Fold each piece in half to make a doubled, 9×12¼-inch rectangle. Score each cover 1 inch from the cut edge to make the spine.

3 To make a window for the front-cover photo, open out one cover and draw a 2¾×3½-inch rectangle centered on the right side (see the photo *top right*). Cut out the window with a crafts knife. Make a ¼-inch slit in the fold for

the ribbon, centering the slit. Thread a 24-inch piece of ribbon through the slit. Glue one end of the ribbon at the back edge of the front cover and leave the remaining end free, beyond the fold (see the photo *top right*).

4 From the black and gold art papers, cut rectangles slightly larger than the family photo; the black rectangle should be larger than the window opening. Use spray adhesive to mount the photo on the gold paper and then attach the gold rectangle to the black one. Center the photo on the left half of the inside front cover over the ribbon, and secure it in the corners with small pieces of tape. Apply spray adhesive to the right inside front cover (the window side), then refold the cover along the fold line and press in place.

5 For the back cover, open out the folded 9×12¼-inch rectangle and cut a slit in the fold at the center to match the slit on the front cover. Thread ribbon through, securing one end at the back edge with a dot of glue. Apply spray adhesive to one side of the inside back cover and press the two sides together.

6 To make the leather spine wrap, cut a 2¾×9-inch rectangle from soft leather or suede. Make a template for punching the holes from a 1×9-inch piece of heavy paper. Use the hole punch to make holes 1½ inches from the top and bottom edges and ½ inch in from one long edge of the template. Attach the template to one long edge of the leather spine wrap and punch two holes; repeat for the opposite edge.

7 Working with one page or envelope at a time, clip the template to the folded tab edge of each sheet of paper and the bottom of each envelope, and punch the holes.

8 To assemble the album, stack the back cover, pages, envelopes, and front cover, lining up the holes. Wrap the spine with the leather strip, aligning the holes. Using a crochet hook, pull an O ring through each hole, then push a rod through the O rings on the front and back of the album. The rod and O rings hold the book together and can be disassembled if you want to add more pages.

137

◀ It's the next best thing to being there. Keep in touch with faraway friends with a gift pack of stationery supplies, such as note paper, postcards, postage stamps, a pen, and sealing wax and a stamp. Also include a prepaid phone card, available from post offices, grocery stores, and discount stores.

In a Twinkling: Instant Gifts

▲ Present a bouquet of memories with film, an album, storage box, and frame. For the film "flowers," cut a ⅛-inch-diameter dowel into 10-inch lengths, and paint each one green. Use a crafts knife or paring knife to make a small slit in the bottom of each plastic film container. Slip a dowel through the slit and into the center of the roll of film.

◀ For friends headed to the beach or on a cruise, fill a straw hat with sunglasses, magazines or books about their destination, sun block, a disposable camera (panoramic for scenic areas, underwater for scuba divers, or outdoors for the beach), and a travel umbrella for an occasional rainy day.

Inspire a would-be gardener with a pot full of gardening tools and supplies, such as a trowel, pruning shears, gloves, and seed packets for the coming season. For an indoor gardener, fill a terra-cotta saucer with gravel or small pebbles, add a few narcissus bulbs, and wrap the saucer in clear cellophane. Remember to include instructions for forcing: Place the saucer in a sunny spot and add water to just below the base of the bulbs. Keep the water at this level.

Encourage a budding artist with a gift certificate for a class at your local art center or art museum. Assemble the certificate, a class schedule, and a few supplies, and present them on a "palette" made from cardboard (a pizza box works well) and covered with a second copy of the class schedule. Cut two slits in the palette and thread a ribbon through to tie the supplies in place.

Please a pet owner (or the owner's pet) with a new bowl and an assortment of pet treats, toys, grooming supplies, and even a new leash.

Pomegranate
Vinegar

Lemon-and-Basil
Vinegar

Orange-Pistachio
Muffin Mix
(see recipe,
page 142)

Almond-Chocolate
Cups (see recipe,
page 143)

Gifts from the kitchen are sure to please almost everyone on your list. Choose salty or sweet, according to each person's tastes.

culinary christmas

Lemon-and-Basil Vinegar

Combined with a splash of olive oil, this makes a delicious low-fat salad dressing.

- 1 cup tightly packed fresh basil leaves
- 4 cups white vinegar or white wine vinegar
- 2 cups dry white wine
- 3 cloves garlic, minced
- ½ lemon

Wash the basil leaves and pat dry with paper towels. In a medium stainless steel or glass saucepan combine basil, vinegar, wine, and garlic. Use a vegetable peeler to remove the yellow portion of the lemon peel in narrow strips and add the strips to the saucepan. (Juice lemon for another purpose.) Bring the mixture almost to boiling. Remove from heat and cover loosely with 100% cotton cheesecloth; set aside to cool to room temperature. Pour into 2 clean 1-quart glass jars.

Cover jars tightly with a nonmetallic lid (or cover the jar with plastic wrap and seal with a metal lid). Let mixture stand in a cool, dark place for 2 weeks. When ready to bottle the vinegar for gifts, line a colander with several thicknesses of 100% cotton cheesecloth. Pour vinegar mixture through the colander and let it drain into a bowl. Discard solids. Transfer strained vinegar to clean, glass bottles. If desired, add a rinsed and dried sprig of basil and a narrow strip or two of lemon peel to each bottle.

Cover bottle with a nonmetallic lid (or cover with plastic wrap and tightly seal with a metal lid). Store in a cool, dark place up to 6 months. Makes 5½ cups.

POMEGRANATE VINEGAR: Prepare Lemon and Basil Vinegar, omitting the basil and garlic. Cut 1 or 2 pomegranates in half through the skin. Remove the peel and break the fruit into sections. Separate the seeds from the membrane; discard membrane. You should have ¾ to 1¼ cups seeds. Press seeds slightly with a potato masher in a large stainless steel or glass saucepan, releasing juices. Add the vinegar, wine, and lemon peel strips. Continue with recipe as directed. If desired, add a few additional pomegranate seeds along with a strip or two of lemon peel to each bottle.

Nutrition facts per tablespoon: 5 cal., 0 g total fat (0 g sat. fat), 0 mg chol., 0 mg sodium, 1 g carbo., 0 g fiber, 0 g pro. Daily values: 0% vit. A, 0% vit. C, 0% calcium, 0% iron

here's how...

To present flavored vinegar, wash decorative bottles in hot soapy water and rinse thoroughly. After they've dried, use thick white crafts glue to attach small craft jewels around the neck and down the front, forming a grapelike cluster. Fill the bottles with vinegar and tie two small Christmas balls around the neck of the bottle with fine gold cording. Add a decorative gift tag.

Pear-Cranberry Conserve
(*see recipe*, page 144)

Hot Fudge Sauce

Caramel-Rum Sauce

Stir in cream, water, and corn syrup. Cook and stir over medium heat until thickened and bubbly (mixture may look curdled). Cook and stir 2 minutes more. Remove from heat. Stir in butter, rum, and vanilla. Let mixture stand at room temperature until cool.

FOR GIFT GIVING: Pour into half-pint jars. Seal and label. Store sauce in the refrigerator up to 2 months. Makes 4 half-pints (about 3½ cups).

Nutrition facts per tablespoon: 52 cal., 1 g total fat (1 g sat. fat), 4 mg chol., 15 mg sodium, 9 g carbo., 0 g fiber, 0 g pro. Daily values: 1% vit. A, 0% vit. C, 1% calcium, 1% iron

Orange-Pistachio Muffin Mix

This recipe makes two batches of muffin mix (see photo, page 140).

    3 cups all-purpose flour
    1 cup sugar
    ½ cup nonfat dry milk powder
    4 teaspoons baking powder
    2 teaspoons dried grated
          orange peel
    ¾ teaspoon salt
    ⅔ cup shortening (that does not
          need refrigeration)
    1 cup chopped pistachios or
          toasted almonds

Combine flour, sugar, milk powder, baking powder, orange peel, and salt in an extra-large mixing bowl. Using a pastry blender, cut in shortening until mixture resembles coarse crumbs. Stir in nuts. Divide mixture in half (each about 3⅓ cups) and place in 2 airtight containers or self-sealing storage bags. Store up to 6 weeks at room temperature or 6 months in the freezer. Each mix makes 12 muffins.

TO BAKE MUFFINS FROM ONE MIX: Place one mix in a large mixing bowl. Make a well in the center of the dry mixture. Combine 1 beaten egg and

Hot Fudge Sauce

    8 ounces semisweet chocolate
          pieces (1⅓ cups)
    ½ cup butter
    1⅓ cups sugar
    1⅓ cups whipping cream

Melt chocolate and butter in a heavy medium saucepan over low heat, stirring frequently. Add sugar. Gradually add whipping cream. Bring to boiling; reduce heat. Boil gently over low heat for 8 minutes, stirring frequently. Remove from heat. Let stand at room temperature until cool.

FOR GIFT GIVING: Pour into half-pint jars. Seal and label. Store sauce in the refrigerator up to 2 months. On the gift tag or label, include directions to reheat the fudge sauce in a small saucepan over medium-low heat and serve over ice cream. Makes 4 half-pints (about 3½ cups).

Nutrition facts per tablespoon: 71 cal., 5 g total fat (2 g sat. fat), 12 mg chol., 19 mg sodium, 8 g carbo., 0 g fiber, 0 g pro. Daily values: 3% vit. A, 0% vit. C, 0% calcium, 0% iron

Caramel-Rum Sauce

Pair a jar of this sauce with one of the Hot Fudge Sauce for a double treat.

    2 cups packed brown sugar
    ¼ cup cornstarch
    1⅓ cups half-and-half or light cream
    1 cup water
    ½ cup light-colored corn syrup
    ¼ cup butter
    ¼ cup rum
    2 teaspoons vanilla

Combine brown sugar and cornstarch in a heavy large saucepan.

¾ cup water in a small bowl. Add all at once to the dry mixture. Stir just until moistened (batter should be somewhat lumpy). Spoon into twelve 2½-inch greased or paper bake cup-lined muffin cups, filling each ⅔ full. Sprinkle lightly with a mixture of 1 tablespoon sugar and ⅛ teaspoon ground nutmeg.

Bake in a 375° oven for 20 to 25 minutes or until golden. Cool in muffin cups on wire rack for 5 minutes. Remove muffins; serve warm.

FOR GIFT GIVING: Label each package and include baking directions. To wrap the gift, see the packaging idea *below*.

Nutrition facts per muffin: 182 cal., 9 g total fat (2 g sat. fat), 18 mg chol., 141 mg sodium, 23 g carbo., 1 g fiber, 4 g pro. Daily values: 1% vit. A, 2% vit. C, 7% calcium, 7% iron

how...

To package Orange-Pistachio Muffin Mix for gift giving, center one bag of mix on a square of green cellophane (available from crafts stores and art supply stores). Pull the cellophane up around the bag and secure it with a rubber band. Cut a square of white tulle 2 to 3 inches larger than the cellophane square. Center the cellophane-wrapped muffin mix on the tulle and tie the tulle with a bow. Attach purchased snowflake stickers to the tulle. Present the mix with a cast-iron or novelty muffin pan.

Almond-Chocolate Cups

Look for small foil candy cups at gourmet cooking shops or paper-supply stores (see photo, page 140).

 1 3-ounce package cream
        cheese, softened
 ¼ to ½ teaspoon almond extract
 3 cups sifted powdered sugar

 ¼ cup finely chopped
        toasted almonds
 1 12-ounce package (2 cups)
        semisweet chocolate pieces
 16 ounces chocolate-flavored
        candy coating, cut up
        Small foil candy cups

Beat cream cheese and almond extract in a medium mixing bowl until smooth. Gradually add powdered sugar, stirring until mixture is thoroughly combined. (If necessary, knead in the last of the powdered sugar by hand.) Stir or knead in chopped almonds.

Divide mixture into four equal portions. On a cutting board roll one portion at a time to a 12-inch-long rope; cut crosswise into ½-inch pieces. Cover with plastic wrap to prevent drying out as you work with candy.

Melt together chocolate pieces and candy coating in a heavy medium saucepan over low heat, stirring just until smooth. Remove from heat. Place foil cups in large shallow pan. Spoon some of the melted chocolate mixture into one-fourth of the candy cups, filling each cup about ⅔ full.

Press a piece of cheese mixture in center of each cup (chocolate will not completely cover the cheese mixture). Repeat with remaining filling and chocolate, working with one-fourth at a time. If chocolate starts to set up, reheat over low heat just until smooth. Drizzle any remaining chocolate over white portion of candies, if desired.

Set cups aside until firm at room temperature (about 30 minutes) or in refrigerator about 10 minutes. Store in a tightly covered container in the refrigerator. Makes about 96 pieces.

FOR GIFT GIVING: Arrange candy cups in a box or decorative plate with instructions to store in the refrigerator.

Nutrition facts per piece: 60 cal., 3 g total fat (2 g sat. fat), 1 mg chol., 3 mg sodium, 9 g carbo., 0 g fiber, 0 g pro. Daily values: 0% vit. A, 0% vit. C, 0% calcium, 0% iron

Sugar Cookie Snowflakes

 ⅓ cup butter
 ⅓ cup shortening
 ¾ cup sugar
 1 teaspoon baking powder
 1 egg
 1 tablespoon milk
 1 teaspoon vanilla
 2 cups all-purpose flour
        Powdered Sugar Glaze
        Decorations (optional)

Beat butter and shortening with an electric mixer on medium to high speed 30 seconds. Add sugar, baking powder, and dash salt; beat well. Add egg, milk, and vanilla; beat until well combined. Beat in as much flour as you can. Stir in any remaining flour. Divide dough in half. Wrap; chill dough for 3 hours.

Roll half of the dough at a time ⅛ inch thick on a lightly floured surface. Cut with 3- to 3½-inch cookie cutters into 6- or 8-pointed star shapes or scalloped rounds. Using tiny hors d'oeuvres cutters or a sharp knife, cut small shapes from cutouts to make snowflake designs. Place on ungreased cookie sheet. Bake in a 375° oven for 7 to 8 minutes or until edges are firm and bottoms are very lightly browned. Transfer to a wire rack and cool.

To decorate, dip tops in Powdered Sugar Glaze. If desired, sprinkle with edible glitter, colored decorating sugar, and/or tiny white decorative candies. Makes 36 to 48 cookies.

POWDERED SUGAR GLAZE: Stir together 1 cup sifted powdered sugar, ¼ teaspoon vanilla, and milk (3 to 4 teaspoons) to make glazing consistency.

FOR GIFT GIVING: See *page 71* for a packaging idea.

Nutrition facts per cookie: 85 cal., 4 g total fat (2 g sat. fat), 11 mg chol., 33 mg sodium, 12 g carbo., 0 g fiber, 1 g pro. Daily values: 1% vit. A, 0% vit. C, 1% calcium, 2% iron

143

Pesto Popcorn Seasoning Mix

milk, oil, lemon peel, and almond extract in a medium mixing bowl; mix well. Add all at once to the dry mixture. Stir just until moistened (batter should be lumpy). Fold in cherries and nuts. Spoon into prepared muffin cups, dividing batter evenly (cups will be full). **Bake in a 400° oven** for 12 to 15 minutes or until golden brown. Cool in muffin cups on wire rack for 5 minutes. Remove muffins. Brush lightly with Lemon Glaze. Makes 36. **LEMON GLAZE:** Stir together ¾ cup sifted powdered sugar, 2 teaspoons lemon juice, and enough water (2 to 3 teaspoons) to make a glaze. **FOR GIFT GIVING:** Prepare and bake muffins as directed; cool completely. Do not glaze. Place in a freezer container or bag; freeze for up to 3 months. Before serving or giving as a gift, remove from freezer and thaw at room temperature. Prepare Lemon Glaze; brush muffins lightly with glaze.

Nutrition facts per muffin: 91 cal., 4 g total fat (1 g sat. fat), 14 mg chol., 42 mg sodium, 13 g carbo., 0 g fiber, 2 g pro. Daily values: 3% vit. A, 0% vit. C, 2% calcium, 2% iron

Pesto Popcorn Seasoning Mix

Give this seasoning mix with a jar of unpopped popcorn—see pages 128–29 for a packaging idea.

    3 tablespoons butter-flavored
         sprinkles
    2 tablespoons grated
         Parmesan cheese
    1 teaspoon dried basil, crushed
    ½ teaspoon dried parsley flakes,
         crushed
    ⅛ to ¼ teaspoon garlic powder

Combine all ingredients in a small bowl. Store mix in the refrigerator. Seasoning mixture will coat about 10 cups of popped popcorn. **FOR GIFT GIVING:** Pour the seasoning mix into a 4-ounce-size bottle. Include instructions to keep refrigerated.

Nutrition facts for entire seasoning mix: 133 cal., 4 g total fat (2 g sat. fat), 10 mg chol., 1,853 mg sodium, 19 g carbo., 0 g fiber, 5 g pro. Daily values: 3% vit. A, 1% vit. C, 15% calcium, 3% iron

Sour Cream-Cherry Muffins

Only one mini-muffin pan? Keep the remaining batter refrigerated while baking each batch (see photo, page 145).

    2 cups all-purpose flour
    ½ cup sugar
    2 teaspoons baking powder
    ¼ teaspoon salt
    2 eggs
    ½ cup dairy sour cream
    ½ cup milk
    ¼ cup cooking oil
    ½ teaspoon finely shredded
         lemon peel
    ¼ teaspoon almond extract
    1 cup dried tart red cherries,
         coarsely chopped
    ½ cup chopped almonds
       Lemon Glaze

Grease thirty-six 1¾-inch muffin cups or line with miniature paper bake cups. Stir together flour, sugar, baking powder, and salt in a large mixing bowl. Make a well in the center of the dry mixture. Combine eggs, sour cream,

Pear-Cranberry Conserve

Try this freezer spread on toasted English muffins (see photo, page 142).

    1 cup cranberries
    ½ cup water
    6½ cups sugar
    1½ to 2 pounds pears, cored,
         peeled, and finely chopped
         (3 cups)
    ¾ cup finely chopped
         walnuts or pecans
    2 teaspoons finely shredded
         lemon peel
    1 6-ounce package liquid
         fruit pectin (2 foil pouches)
    ⅓ cup lemon juice

Combine cranberries and water in a 4-quart Dutch oven. Bring to boiling. Cover and cook for 2 minutes or until cranberries begin to pop. Stir in sugar; gently simmer for 10 minutes or until sugar dissolves. Remove from heat. Add pears, nuts, and lemon peel. Let stand 10 minutes, stirring occasionally. Combine pectin and lemon juice in a mixing bowl; add to pear mixture. Stir 3 minutes. Ladle at once into clean, half-pint jars or freezer containers, leaving ½-inch headspace. Seal and label. Let stand for several hours until set. Store up to 3 weeks in the refrigerator or 1 year in the freezer. Makes 8 half-pints.

FOR THE GIFT TAG: Keep conserve frozen until ready to use; thaw in the refrigerator overnight before serving.

Nutrition facts per tablespoon: 54 cal., 1 g total fat (0 g sat. fat), 0 mg chol., 0 mg sodium, 13 g carbo., 0 g fiber, 0 g pro. Daily values: 0% vit. A, 1% vit. C, 0% calcium, 0% iron

Coffeehouse Chocolate Spoons

Sour Cream-Cherry Muffins

Coffeehouse Chocolate Spoons

Use plastic spoons or collect metal spoons from flea markets or antique shops to make these flavorful gifts.

    6 ounces semisweet
        chocolate pieces
    4 ounces milk chocolate pieces
        or white baking bar
20 to 24 spoons

Place semisweet chocolate pieces in a heavy saucepan over low heat, stirring constantly until the chocolate begins to melt. Immediately remove from heat and stir until chocolate is smooth. Dip spoons into chocolate, draining off excess chocolate (see photo, *right*). Place spoons on waxed paper; refrigerate for 30 minutes to allow chocolate to set up.

Place milk chocolate pieces or white baking bar in a heavy saucepan over low heat, stirring constantly until chocolate begins to melt. Immediately remove from heat and stir until smooth. Cool to room temperature. Place the melted chocolate in a small self-sealing plastic bag. Using scissors, make a small cut in the corner of the bag; drizzle one or both sides of the chocolate-coated spoons with the melted milk chocolate or white baking bar. Refrigerate spoons for 30 minutes to allow chocolate to set up.

FOR GIFT GIVING: Wrap each spoon separately and store in a cool dry place for 2 to 3 weeks until ready to give as gifts. If desired, bundle a week's worth in a jumbo holiday coffee mug. Makes 20 to 24 spoons.

Nutrition facts per spoon: 69 cal., 4 g total fat (3 g sat. fat), 0 mg chol., 6 mg sodium, 8 g carbo., 1 g fiber, 1 g pro. Daily values: 0% vit. A, 0% vit. C, 1% calcium, 2% iron

here's how...

For chocolate-coated spoons: Dip a plastic or metal spoon into the melted semisweet chocolate. Tap the handle of the spoon on the edge of the saucepan to remove excess chocolate. Place spoons on a tray lined with waxed paper and chill until set.

If your youngsters are bouncing off the walls in anticipation of the holidays, channel their energy into something creative. Making crafts, cookies, and candy (with an adult's help, when necessary) not only keeps kids busy, but also encourages them to think about sharing: Show them how to make gifts for their friends and family, and you reinforce the season's message of remembering others. Cooking and crafting also build self-esteem, as long as you don't insist on perfection, and these activities let kids take pride in contributing to the family decorations or dessert table. Best of all, when you spend time with your children, making treats for the birds or paper-star garlands for the tree, you build loving memories that last well beyond the season.

STUFF

Keep little hands busy before the holidays by making ornaments, cards, and treats from the kitchen. Crafts give kids of all ages an opportunity to share the spirit of the season.

crafts *for* kids

Ice-Cream Ornaments

Glue glass balls into real sugar cones to make these Christmas confections for the tree.

here's how...

1 For each ornament, spray the cone with two or more coats of clear spray varnish and let it dry. Glue the ornament into the cone so the hanger is centered on the top.

2 String jute or twine between two chairs to hang the ornaments for painting, and protect the floor with newspapers. Thin the paint with water, if necessary, so it's the consistency of half-and-half cream. Starting at the hanger, spoon paint over the ornament, allowing it to drip like chocolate sauce. Before the paint dries, drop sprinkles over the ornament. The dried paint will hold the sprinkles in place.

SHOPPING LIST

ice-cream cones (sugar or waffle or waffle bowls)
clear spray varnish
plain glass ball ornaments to fit cones
thick white crafts glue
acrylic paint (brown and white)
plastic spoons for the paint
sprinkles (from the cake decorating section of a grocery store)

Hanukkah Card

This card doubles as a gift—there's a dreidel game inside for kids to play with their friends.

here's how...

1 Cut the paper to 5½x9 inches and fold it in half to make a 4½x5½-inch card. Referring to the photo for help, stamp the front of the card with the Hanukkah and dreidel stamps. Let the ink dry about 10 minutes.

2 Use the fine-tip markers and a ruler to draw a double border around the front of the card.

3 On the inside of the card, copy the Hebrew symbols shown *at right*, drawing one symbol on each edge of the card as shown. Also draw a border around the "game board."

4 To make the spinner, stamp the dreidel image on a scrap of watercolor paper, and cut an arrow shape around it. To find the center of the game board, measure the width and divide it in half; do the same for the length. Cut a small hole in the center and attach the spinner with the paper fastener. Attach the fastener loosely enough to allow the spinner to move when you flick it with your fingers.

nun: wins nothing

gimmel: wins everything in the "pot"

hay: wins half the "pot"

shin: puts one into the "pot"

family traditions

Because Hanukkah is actually a relatively minor festival in Judaism, and Christmas is so central to Christianity, there really should be no comparison between the two; but because they occur so close together and because of the marketing hype surrounding Christmas, children can sometimes feel left out. To counter this in our home, we play Hanukkah music tapes in the car while running errands and we put up colorful streamers and stars around the house. We always try to make charity part of the Hanukkah experience, too—the children use their own money to buy toys, which we then donate to Toys for Tots.

— *Paula Rudofsky*
Mount Kisco, New York

Holiday Greetings

Send greetings from the group with this card. It's a good project for a class or youth group.

SHOPPING LIST

From a crafts store:
- 8×11-inch sheets of heavy green paper (such as charcoal paper)
- rubber stamps
- clear rubber stamp ink
- Winter Wonderland opaque embossing powder
- electric embossing tool
- glue sticks
- envelopes to fit card (about 4¾×5¾ inches)
- pencil, ruler, and scissors
- adhesive tape
- color photocopies of photos

~ Make as many photocopies of the collage of faces as you have children in your group and have each child decorate and assemble a card. Deliver the cards to nursing home residents or children in the hospital over the holidays, or send cards to speakers or visitors who have led field trips or enrichment classes for the group during the year.

here's how...

1 For each card, fold a sheet of paper into thirds across the 11-inch width. Trim the card's height to 5½ inches.

2 Open out the card and draw a simple tree shape in the center of the middle section. Cut out the tree.

151

3 Turn the card over and use rubber stamps to add a greeting below the tree and a star to the top. To make embossed images, press the rubber stamp onto a rubber-stamp pad inked with clear ink. Press the stamp firmly on the paper, then sprinkle embossing powder over the image.

4 Shake off the excess powder. If you're working with children under age 10, you'll need to melt the powder for them, using an electric embossing tool. Older children can do this themselves, with supervision.

5 To make the collage of faces, first make color copies of the children's faces. Tape as many photos as will fit onto an 8½×11-inch piece of paper and make a copy, then cut out the faces and arrange them to fit inside the tree shape. Copy as many as you need for cards made from this collage.

6 Position the color copy behind the tree cutout and secure it with adhesive tape. With the back of the collage facing you, fold the left section of the card over to cover the back of the collage and glue it in place. Add a message on the right section (the inside of the card) from the class.

For the Birds

Remember our feathered and furry friends with these winter treats.

sunflower-seed hearts

Use a heart-shaped cookie cutter to cut shapes from stale bread. Make a hole in the top and thread raffia or twine through it to make a hanger. Cover the shape with peanut butter, then push sunflower seeds and other birdseed into the peanut butter.

orange baskets

Scoop out the pulp from an orange half. Pierce a hole near the rim on each side and thread a piece of raffia through each hole. Knot each piece, then tie them together to make a hanger. Fill the basket with dried cranberries and raisins.

SHOPPING LIST

- heart-shaped cookie cutter
- stale bread
- peanut butter
- sunflower seeds or mixed birdseed
- twine or raffia
- oranges, raisins, dried cranberries, and apples
- dried corn cobs

fruits and veggies

Cut thin slices of apples and oranges and hang them outdoors with raffia loops. Buy cobs of dried corn from a birdfood-supply shop, slice them into sections, and hang each section from a tree branch with a raffia loop.

Handmade-Paper Star Garland

This elegant-looking garland is easier to make than you might think.

Start with an ordinary papermaking kit, available at crafts stores, to make these paper stars. Use an old blender to make the pulp. Add gold glitter to the pulp, then press it into a sheet following the kit manufacturer's instructions, and let it dry.

Use a cookie cutter to trace stars on the paper and cut them out. String gold beads onto sewing thread or heavy carpet thread, adding a star every few inches. To attach each star, take a stitch in one point, knot the thread, and cut it. Make a stitch in the opposite point and continue adding beads.

Marbleized-Paper Ornaments

Liquid starch and acrylic paints make this ancient
craft accessible to kids—and adults.

SHOPPING LIST

From a crafts store:

acrylic paint in any color
2 sheets of white
   construction paper
tracing paper
ribbon or braid
   for hanger
glue stick
distilled water
plastic spoon
paper cup
liquid starch
9×13-inch baking pan
large-toothed comb
   or a feather

here's how...

1 Use the plastic spoon to mix
2 tablespoons of paint with 2 tablespoons of distilled water in a paper cup.
Add more paint or water as necessary to
make a creamy mixture.

2 Pour enough starch into the baking
pan to measure 1 to 1½ inches deep.
Skim the surface with a paper towel to
remove any air bubbles.

153

3
Dribble several
drops of the paint
mixture onto the
starch. If the paint
sinks below the
starch surface, add
a little more
distilled water to
the paint and
dribble a few
more drops onto
the starch. Use a
comb or feather to
swirl the paint on
the surface.

4
Lay a sheet of construction
paper on top of the paint,
letting the middle of the page
touch first. After about 15 seconds, lift the paper from the
paint. Lay it, paint side up, on
paper towels.

5 Lay a paper towel on
top of the paper. With the
heel of your hand, press
down on the paper towel to
remove excess
paint. Pull off the
paper towel and
repeat with anoth-
er paper towel.
Lay aside the
marbled paper,
paint side up, and
let it dry. Repeat
this procedure to marbleize a
second sheet of paper.

6 To make the ornaments,
draw a star, tree, or bell
shape onto tracing paper; cut
it out. Rub the glue stick over
the unpainted side of one
sheet of marbled paper; press
it to the unpainted side of the
remaining sheet.

7 Trace the
pattern twice onto
the marbled paper and cut out the
shapes. Starting from the bottom of one
cutout, cut a slit two-thirds of the way up
the shape. Pierce a small hole at the top
of the shape; thread a ribbon hanger
through the hole, and knot the ends.

8 Starting at the top of the second
cutout, cut a slit one-third of the way
down. Hold the shapes perpendicular
to each other, and slip the one with
the hanger over the top of the
second shape.

Candy and Caramel Corn

Marbleized Mint Bark

Visions of Sugar Plums

Kids will have fun helping make these treats for snacking and gift giving.

Candy and Caramel Corn

6 cups popped popcorn
    (about ¼ cup unpopped)
3 tablespoons butter
¼ cup light-colored corn syrup
1 tablespoon molasses
1 cup dry roasted peanuts
1 cup red and green candy-
    coated milk chocolate pieces

Place the popped popcorn in a 15×10×1-inch baking pan. Melt butter in a small saucepan. Remove from heat.
Stir corn syrup and molasses into melted butter. Slowly drizzle the corn syrup mixture over popcorn in baking pan. Using a wooden spoon, toss the popcorn and coat it as evenly as possible with corn syrup mixture.
Bake in a 325° oven for 15 minutes, stirring with a wooden spoon every 5 minutes. Pour caramel corn into a large, nonplastic serving bowl. Stir in peanuts. Let caramel corn cool.
Stir candy-coated pieces into cooled caramel corn. Store in a tightly covered container at room temperature. Makes about 6 cups.

Nutrition facts per ½-cup serving: 202 cal., 12 g total fat (3 g sat. fat), 8 mg chol., 133 mg sodium, 21 g carbo., 1 g fiber, 4 g pro. Daily values: 2% vit. A, 0% vit. C, 1% calcium, 4% iron

Marbleized Mint Bark

Kid's Job: Swirl melted chocolate into the peppermint-dotted candy coating mixture.

⅓ cup mint-flavored semisweet
    chocolate pieces or
    semisweet chocolate pieces
1 pound vanilla-flavored candy
    coating, cut up
¾ cup finely crushed candy cane
    or finely crushed striped
    round peppermint candies

Line a baking sheet with foil; set aside. Heat chocolate pieces in a small saucepan over low heat, stirring constantly, until melted and smooth. Remove pan from heat. Heat the candy coating in a 2-quart saucepan over low heat, stirring constantly, until melted and smooth. Remove pan from heat. Stir in crushed candies. Pour the melted coating mixture onto the prepared baking sheet.
Spread the coating mixture about ⅜ inch thick; drizzle with the melted chocolate. Gently zigzag a narrow metal spatula through the chocolate and peppermint layers to create a swirled effect in the candy.
Let candy stand at room temperature for several hours or until firm. (Or, chill about 30 minutes or until firm.) Use foil to lift candy from the baking sheet and carefully break candy into pieces. Store, tightly covered, for up to 2 weeks. Makes about 1¼ pounds.

Nutrition facts per ounce: 159 cal., 8 g total fat (4 g sat. fat), 1 mg chol., 22 mg sodium, 22 g carbo., 0 g fiber, 2 g pro. Daily values: 0% vit. A, 0% vit. C, 4% calcium, 1% iron

Christmas Tree Brownies

Start with a brownie mix and create festive trees that kids can decorate and offer proudly as gifts for teachers and friends.

1 21½-ounce package fudge
    brownie mix
1 beaten egg
¼ cup cooking oil
¼ cup milk
¼ cup water
¾ cup miniature semisweet
    chocolate pieces or finely
    chopped nuts
    Decorator icing (optional)
    Miniature candy-coated
    semisweet chocolate pieces
    (optional)

Combine brownie mix, egg, oil, milk, and water in a large mixing bowl. Stir in chocolate pieces or nuts just until combined. Spread in a greased 13×9×2-inch baking pan. (If desired, to remove the baked brownies easily from the pan, line the pan with foil, extending the foil over the edges of the pan slightly; grease the foil. Spread batter in pan, bake, and cool. After cooling, lift the baked bars out of the pan and cut into shapes.)

Bake in a 350° oven for 30 minutes. Cool completely in pan on a wire rack.

Cut into triangle shapes. Decorate with decorator icing and miniature candy-coated semisweet chocolate pieces, if desired. Makes 30 trees.

Nutrition facts per brownie: 130 cal., 5 g total fat (1 g sat. fat), 7 mg chol., 80 mg sodium, 21 g carbo., 0 g fiber, 1 g pro. Daily values: 0% vit. A, 0% vit. C, 0% calcium, 4% iron

Rudolph's Peanut Butter Cookies

155

Rudolph's Peanut Butter Cookies

½ cup butter
½ cup peanut butter
½ cup sugar
½ teaspoon baking soda
½ teaspoon baking powder
¼ cup honey
1 egg
½ teaspoon vanilla
1¼ cups all-purpose flour
¾ cup chopped peanuts
80 small pretzels
40 small red gumdrops
    Semisweet chocolate pieces

Beat butter and peanut butter in a large mixing bowl with an electric mixer on medium to high speed for 30 seconds. Add sugar, baking soda, and baking powder and beat until combined. Beat in honey, egg, and vanilla until combined. Beat in as much of the flour as you can with the mixer. Stir in peanuts and any remaining flour with a wooden spoon. Divide dough in half. Wrap in plastic wrap. Chill dough for 1 hour or until easy to handle.

Work with half the dough at a time, keeping the rest refrigerated. Using 1 tablespoon dough for each cookie, shape into a triangle about 2½ inches long and 2 inches wide on an ungreased cookie sheet. Lightly press pretzel antlers into side at wide end of triangles. Add gumdrop noses and chocolate pieces for eyes.

Bake in a 375° oven for 7 to 8 minutes or until bottoms are lightly browned. Cool 2 minutes on cookie sheet. Carefully transfer to a wire rack and cool. Makes about 40 cookies.

Nutrition facts per cookie: 103 cal., 5 g total fat (2 g sat. fat), 11 mg chol., 114 mg sodium, 12 g carbo., 1 g fiber, 2 g pro. Daily values: 2% vit. A, 0% vit. C, 0% calcium, 2% iron

Great Guns

Florists introduced hot-glue guns to the crafting world over a decade ago. Now there's a bewildering variety of guns and glues available. Here's a guide to help you choose.

tools & techniques

The old standby, great for general crafting, is the **high-temperature gun**. The glue, which is actually a wax, gets hot enough to form a strong bond for adhering paper, fabric, jewelry findings, and dried materials. But the heated glue can burn fingers as well as some plastics and fabrics.

Low-temperature guns use oval glue sticks that melt at a lower temperature so you're less likely to burn yourself or damage plastics and fabrics. Their drawbacks: the bond isn't as strong and the glue may remelt if exposed to high heat or direct sunlight.

Dual-temperature guns efficiently go from high to low temp with the flip of a switch. They offer the benefits of both and use either dual-temp (also called high-low) glue sticks that work on both temperatures or high-temp sticks that work only on the glue gun's high setting.

Mini guns are inexpensive (often under $5). While they're good for getting into tiny places and pack well into tool boxes, they don't get hot enough for the glue to produce a strong bond. The glue sticks are more slender than most and you may have to feed them into the gun by pushing the stick with your thumb instead of pulling a trigger.

Cordless guns make it easy to work on projects where there's no electrical outlet handy. Since most types cool down over time, they're best for projects that require short bursts of gluing.

Pan-melt hot glue, also known as a glue pot, is preferred by many florists and professional crafters because for many projects, it's easier to use—you just dip the dried flower, pinecone, or piece of plastic fruit into a pan or pot of melted glue and then press it in place. Some pots have an adapter to melt glue sticks while others use chips or pillows. The glue pillows are waterproof (glue sticks aren't). But they're more likely to soften when exposed to high heat or direct sunlight.

When you buy glue sticks, read the label on the package or the individual glue sticks to make sure the glue matches your gun and meets your needs. Although hot glue generally isn't recommended for wood, new wood-glue sticks on the market can be used on baskets and small projects (see the yellow oval sticks in the photo *above*). Glitter and colored sticks are for decorative use, not as adhesives.

Wiring Know-How

Here are the basic techniques for wiring fruit and pinecones.

〰 Often the best way to secure pinecones and fruit to wreaths and garlands is with floral wire. Use medium- or heavy-gauge wire (florists usually recommend #18 or #19); fine-gauge wire isn't strong enough to support the fruit's weight.

If the fruit can rest flat against the background, you can lighten the weight of the fruit by cutting it in half and scooping out most of the flesh. Push the wire through about ¼ inch from the cut edge (see the photo *top right*).

To wire whole apples, oranges, pears, and lemons, push the wire through the fruit from one side to the other. Pull the wires to the bottom of the fruit and twist them tightly around each other to form a pick. Or, wrap them tightly around a wooden floral pick.

To wire pinecones, simply work the wire around the cone between the two bottom layers of scales. Use needle-nose pliers to tighten and twist the wire, then use the wire ends as a pick to insert into plastic foam or floral foam. If you're adding the cones to a garland or a fresh wreath, push the wires through to the back of the greenery and twist the ends as tightly as necessary to hold the pinecones where you want them.

timesaving tip

■ We store holiday decorations for each room in our house in a separate box. We tape a photograph of the decorated room to the carton and label it. At holiday time, we open the boxes one room at a time, and decorate the house over several days.

——*Cynthia A. Gaitros*
Lynn Haven, Florida

credits & sources

project designers

Page 8: Apples-and-plaids wreath by Aubrey Dunbar, Adel, Iowa.

Pages 10–11: Harvest wreath by Aubrey Dunbar.

Page 28: Miniature bottle with flowers: concept by Charlotte Hagood, Birmingham, Alabama; execution, Jilann Severson, Des Moines; spool tassels by Charlotte Hagood.

Page 29: Pincushion ornament: concept by Charlotte Hagood; execution by Jilann Severson.

Page 39: Candleholder adaptation by Peggy Johnston, Des Moines.

Page 45: Stamped table runner by Peggy Johnston.

Page 46: Place mat pillow and tea towel pillow by Margaret Sindelar, West Des Moines. Offray ribbons available at crafts stores.

Page 47: Lampshade necklace and lampshade crown by Peggy Johnston.

Page 48: Squash votive holder by Joe Ruggiero, Encino, California.

Page 50: Menorah pillow by Jilann Severson; Star of David pillow by Margaret Sindelar.

Pages 52–53: Rosemary topiary and temporary tree by Joe Ruggiero.

Pages 55–56: Planter and windowbox arrangements by Aubrey Dunbar.

Page 58: Chandelier decoration by Sandy Koepke, Beverly Hills, California.

Page 71: Cookie packaging by Carol Field Dahlstrom, Ankeny, Iowa.

Pages 80–81: Centerpiece, chair wreath, votive candleholders by Aubrey Dunbar.

Page 84: Napkin clips, place-card holders and table decoration by Peggy Johnston.

Page 104: Handmade Father Christmas from Red Bear Santas by Carol Carter, Des Moines.

Page 106: Duvets by Sandy Guely, Des Moines. Tartan plaid flannel sheets from The Company Store, 800/285-3696. Spruce green flannel sheets from L.L. Bean, 800/809-7057.

Page 126: Santa's sack by Jilann Severson.

Page 127: Canvas cover-up by Katie Stoddard, Magnolia Springs, Alabama.

Page 132–33: Basket of flowers by Joe Ruggiero.

Page 136: Memory album by Peggy Johnston.

Pages 138–39: Gift ideas by Jilann Severson.

Page 140: Decorative bottles and muffin mix packaging by Carol Field Dahlstrom.

Page 148: Ice-cream ornaments by Jilann Severson.

Pages 150–51: Hanukkah card and holiday greetings card by Barb Vaske, Des Moines.

photographers

Bill Holt: Cover, page 4.

Peter Krumhardt: Pages 8, 10, 11, 17, 19, 28 (top and right), 29 (right), 34 (top), 39 (top and bottom), 41, 43, 44, 45, 46, 47, 50, 51, 55, 56, 57, 59 (bottom left), 60–61, 63, 71, 73, 79, 80, 81, 82 (step-by-step photos), 84, 85 (bottom left and right), 88, 94, 95, 104, 105, 106, 107 (top), 109, 111 (left), 112 (right), 113 (bottom), 114 (right top and bottom), 115 (bottom left and right), 116 (right), 117 (bottom), 126 (right), 127, 136–37, 138–39, 140, 148, 150, 151, 154, 156, 157.

Mark Lohman: Pages 30, 32, 33, 48 (left), 49 (top), 52, 53, 58 (top left), 122, 132, 133.

Bryan McKay: Pages 24 (bottom left and right), 129, 145 (bottom).

photostylists

Jilann Severson: Pages 17, 19, 24, 28 (top and right), 29 (right), 39 (top and bottom), 41, 43, 45, 46 (top and bottom right), 47 (bottom left and right), 51, 79, 82 (center left and right, bottom), 85 (bottom left and right), 126 (right), 127, 129, 136 (bottom), 137, 138–39, 145 (bottom), 148, 150, 151, 156–57.

Peggy Johnston: Pages 9, 34, 44, 46 (top left), 47 (top left and right), 59 (lower left), 84, 136 (top).

Rebecca Jerdee: Pages 94, 104–105, 107 (top).

Jennifer Peterson: Pages 63, 71, 73, 88, 111 (left), 112 (right), 113 (bottom), 114 (top and bottom right), 115 (bottom left and right), 116 (right), 117 (bottom), 140, 154.

recipe development

Linda Henry and **Shelli McConnell**, contributing editors.

158

index

index *continued*